All About Lawns

Created and designed by
the editorial staff of
ORTHO BOOKS

Project Editor
Janet Goldenberg

Writers
Cathy Haas
Michael MacCaskey

Designer
Gary Hespenheide

Ortho Books

Publisher
Robert B. Loperena

Editorial Director
Christine Jordan

Production Director
Ernie S. Tasaki

Managing Editors
Robert J. Beckstrom
Michael D. Smith
Sally W. Smith

System Manager
Linda M. Bouchard

Editorial Assistants
Joni Christiansen
Sally J. French

Address all inquiries to:
Ortho Books
Box 5006
San Ramon, CA 94583-0906

Copyright ©1985, 1994
Monsanto Company
All rights reserved under international and Pan-American copyright conventions.

1 2 3 4 5 6 7 8 9
94 95 96 97 98 99

ISBN 0-89721-265-7
Library of Congress Catalog Card
Number 93-86234

THE SOLARIS GROUP
2527 Camino Ramon
San Ramon, CA 94583

Acknowledgments

Consultants
Dorothy Borland, Turfgrass Consultant, City and County of Denver Parks and Recreation Department, Denver, Colorado
Professor Thomas Cook, Department of Horticulture, Oregon State University, Corvallis, Oregon
Dr. Norman W. Hummel, Jr., Turfgrass Science Program, Cornell University, Ithaca, New York
Mark M. Mahady, Mark M. Mahady & Associates, Pacific Grove, California

Illustrators
Ebet Dudley
Ron Hildebrand
Ronda Hildebrand
Andrea Z. Tachiera

Photography Editor
Roberta Spieckerman

Photo Research Associate
Karen Heilman

Editorial Coordinator
Cass Dempsey

Copyeditor
David Sweet

Proofreaders
Barbara Ferenstein
Fran Taylor

Indexer
Katherine Stimson

Composition by
Laurie A. Steele

Layout & Production by
Indigo Design & Imaging

Separations by
Color Tech Corp.

Lithographed in the USA by
Webcrafters, Inc.

Special Thanks to
Braddock & Logan Associates
Deborah Cowder
Pete Gumas, Sierra Sod and Supply
The Merchant Family
Orchard Supply Nursery
Really Special Plants and Gardens, Berkeley, Calif.
Sequoya Nursery, Oakland, Calif.
Lala Wilson, Pacific Sod

Photographers
Names of photographers are followed by the page numbers on which their work appears.
R=right, C=center, L=left, T=top, B=bottom.

William Aplin: 17L, 18B, 19B
Laurie Black: 40T, 40B, 56TL, 56TR, 56BL, 56BR
Robert J. Black: 39T
A. Boger: 57T, 84TL
Dorothy Borland: 21TR
J. Butler: 87C
Josephine Coatsworth: 49
S. Collman: 88BL
Crandall & Crandall: 57B
A. Crozier: 83TR, 83B, 87T, 88TL
Clyde Elmore: 86B
Dr. M.C. Engelke, Texas A & M University: 20B
Janet Goldenberg: 80
Pete Gumas: 33, 41, 52, 76TL
Dr. Ali Harivandi: 20TL
Saxon Holt: front cover, 4–5, 60, 72R
Michael Landis: title page, 11, 12, 13R, 14R, 15, 16T, 16B, 18T, 19T, 46–47, 51T, 55, 72L, 73L, 73R, 83C, 84BR, 108
Mark M. Mahady: 7, 39B, 67, 76B, back cover BR
Elvin McDonald: 74, 78–79
Michael McKinley: 76TR
J.R. Natter: 89L, 89R
Ortho Photo Library: 24, 50, 73L, 73R, 77L, 83C, 84TR, 84BR, 85T, 85B, 86C, 88R, 108
Pam Peirce: 13L, 14L, 83TL, 84BL
Mike Smith: 86T
Avril R. Stark: 87B, 90
Glenn Steiner: 22–23, 29, 31, 37TL, 37TR, 37BL, 37BR, 38T, 38B, 42, 44T, 44B, 45T, 45B, back cover TL & TR
The Toro Company: back cover BL

Manufacturers
Cushman, Inc., A Ransomes America Corporation Company: 77R
Deere & Company: 62
Homelite, Division of Textron, Inc.: 66L, 66R
The Irrometer Company: 51B
The Toro Company: 48

Gardeners/Landscapers
A to Z Tree Nursery: 29, 31, 37TL, 37TR, 37BL, 37BR, 38T, 38B
Jim Hanson/Ecoscapes, Martinez, Calif: 4–5
Pacific Sod: 29, 31, 37TL, 37TR, 37BL, 37BR, 38T, 38B
Town & Country Landscaping: 29, 31, 37TL, 37TR, 37BL, 37BR, 38T, 38B

Front Cover
A well-planned lawn sets off flower borders, provides walking and playing space, and offers a serene expanse of green—all without being too large for easy care.

Title Page
Stepping-stones lead across a lawn.

Back Cover
Top left: Shaded lawns need special care to stay healthy.

Top right: Sod should be laid parallel to a straight edge, such as this walk.

Bottom left: A mower can be used without a collection bag to return clippings to the lawn. Clippings release nutrients as they decompose, reducing the need for fertilizer.

Bottom right: Tall fescue makes a drought-tolerant lawn that remains lush and green in dry climates.

All About Lawns

What Kind of Lawn for You?

Whether you are planting a new lawn or replacing an old one, there are many kinds of lawns from which to choose.

L awns are different things to different people. To some, a lawn is a pleasant backdrop for a home and its surrounding flowers, trees, and shrubs. To others, a lawn is an outdoor room during warm weather, a place for family activities or quiet times alone.

No matter what role a lawn plays in your life, you are probably aware that having one has both advantages and disadvantages. On the plus side, most lawn grasses are tough, practical plants that can stand repeated trampling and frequent mowing. They grow quickly, and once established they can live for years. Lawns also benefit their environment, generating oxygen, trapping dust and pollutants, and cooling the air through evaporation.

Yet lawns are also demanding. Because they consist of many plants crowded together, their roots penetrating only a few inches into the soil, lawns need frequent and abundant watering. In drought-prone areas, this can tax the local water supply. Most lawns also have large appetites for fertilizer, requiring more per square yard than any other type of planting. And lawns take time to care for. Even if you maintain your lawn at a minimal level, you must find the time to mow, weed, and fertilize it regularly.

Happily, there are many styles of lawns and varieties of lawn grasses from which to choose. Each one offers advantages for a particular environment, maintenance level, or use. By knowing what you need and planning wisely, you can easily make your lawn an enjoyable, trouble-free part of your life.

A well-maintained backyard lawn makes a pleasant outdoor playroom for children.

SELECTING A GRASS

Most homes sold today come with a lawn already in place, so starting one from scratch is seldom necessary. But the lawn that came with your house may be poorly adapted to the climate or beset by environmental problems such as bad drainage or too much shade. Your lawn may have been severely neglected by a previous owner, or it may have been disturbed beyond repair by a building or landscaping project. Or you may wish to use your lawn for a different purpose than the one for which it was intended. For these reasons or for others, you may decide to install a new lawn.

Your first and most important task is to choose a grass that suits your climate and soil. If you live in a cold climate, you will need to plant one of the cool-season grasses, which survive the winter by going dormant; in warm zones you will probably choose one of the warm-season grasses, which can tolerate extended periods of high temperature. Grasses also vary in their tolerance of shade, so if your yard is covered with trees, you should grow a shade-tolerant lawn. If you live in a drought-prone area, look for a grass that can tolerate long periods between waterings.

You will also need to think about how much time and energy you can devote to lawn care. If you want a carefree lawn, choose a grass that resists pests, diseases, and drought; grows slowly; and demands little fertilizing. Grasses meeting these requirements include bermudagrass, a warm-season grass, and certain fescues, which are cool-season grasses. If you will be hiring a professional to care for your lawn, you might opt for a better-looking, higher-maintenance grass than you would choose if you intended to care for the lawn yourself. For example, you might choose bentgrass or a Kentucky bluegrass mixture, both of which are cool-season grasses.

If you are planning to sell your home or need to spruce it up for a special occasion, you will probably want a grass that establishes itself quickly. You can rapidly improve the quality of an existing lawn by overseeding it with a fast-germinating grass such as annual or perennial ryegrass or turf-type tall fescue (for cool-season areas), or bermudagrass (for warm-season areas). If you need to start a lawn quickly from bare ground, sod is the fastest way to accomplish this. The lawn looks good

instantly and is established enough to walk on within three weeks.

You should also determine how your lawn will be used. Do you need to provide a durable play area for children? If so, you should choose a grass that is soft in texture but resistant to wear. The best cool-season grasses, in descending order of wear tolerance, are perennial ryegrass, turf-type tall fescue, Kentucky bluegrass, bentgrass, and fine fescues. The best warm-season grasses, also in descending order of wear tolerance, are zoysiagrass, hybrid bermudagrass, bahiagrass, and common bermudagrass. Be warned, however, that zoysiagrass has needle-sharp leaf tips, making it an uncomfortable choice where people lie on the grass or go barefoot.

Do you want a lawn with a manicured look? Fine-textured types such as bentgrass or fine fescues (for cool-season areas) and hybrid bermudagrass (for warm-season areas) are usually grown for this purpose.

Some kinds of lawn are more costly to maintain than others. Lawn grasses that require a lot of fertilizer or weed killer to look their best, or that need frequent doses of pesticide or fungicide, can be decidedly less economical—especially in warm climates where these materials must be applied throughout the year.

You must also weigh the cost of the various methods of installation. Lawns planted from seed are the least expensive to establish but also the most labor intensive. Plugs or sprigs are next in terms of expense and convenience, followed by sod, which is the most costly but also the quickest to establish.

In choosing a grass, you will probably find that you must make some trade-offs. For example, you may want a fine-textured lawn that requires little maintenance. Unfortunately, few grasses are both fine textured and low maintenance. One solution might be to plant the front yard with the fine-textured grass and the backyard with a more carefree, rougher-textured variety. On the other hand, some grasses can solve more than one problem. For example, a lawn of turf-type tall fescue is both drought tolerant and resistant to foot traffic. The Lawn Grass Comparisons chart on page 21 will help you compare the traits of common lawn grasses.

Of course, a new lawn is not necessarily the answer. If your lawn has been faring poorly, a

simple change in your lawn care practices may be all it takes to solve the problem. See the third chapter for a discussion of lawn care, and the fourth chapter for problem-solving tips.

ANATOMY AND GROWTH

The grasses we use today for lawns evolved in sun-filled prairies and meadows, where they were grazed by large animals. The densely formed grasses that survived in these ecosystems had growing points so low that grazers did not eat them.

Today, the descendants of these grasses exist as dense, low-growing plants that, when grown together, are called lawns. Present lawn grasses tolerate the lawn mower as if it were a grazing animal. Although few people care what individual grass plants look like, an examination of them can reveal a great deal about how a lawn will behave.

Lawn grasses grow from the *crown,* or growing point, which lies next to the ground. As long as the crown is not injured, the plant tolerates having its blades cut without pausing in its growth.

Below the crown is an underground system of fibrous *roots.* The roots absorb water and nutrients and anchor the plant.

Extending upward from the crown is the *primary shoot.* This is the first stem that develops from a seedling. It consists of the blades, collar, sheath, nodes, and internodes.

The *blade* and the *sheath* together make up the leaf. As the plant grows, the sheath remains wrapped around the stem while the blade flattens out and points upward. The *collar* is a narrow band that marks the spot where the sheath and blade meet.

Blades and sheaths originate from *nodes,* bulbous joints in the crown. The portions of

Turf-type tall fescue tolerates heavy foot traffic and infrequent watering, making it ideal for this curbside setting.

stem between nodes are the *internodes.* Several blades, sheaths, nodes, and internodes can exist on a primary shoot; nodes and internodes are also present on spreading stems.

Tillers, which are shoots that grow from the crown beside the primary shoot, make a lawn thick and full. Although tiller growth is apparent in all grasses, bunch grasses have especially heavy tiller activity. Bunch grasses, such as chewings fescue, hard fescue, turf-type tall fescue, and the ryegrasses, form clumps that expand to fill a lawn. Creeping grasses spread by stems that extend from the parent plant. *Rhizomes* are creeping stems that travel below the ground and *stolons* (or *runners*) are those that travel above the ground. Some creeping grasses, such as Kentucky bluegrass and red fescue, spread by rhizomes; some, such as centipedegrass and St. Augustine grass, spread by stolons; and others, such as bermudagrass and zoysiagrass, spread by rhizomes and stolons.

Both rhizomes and stolons produce new plants as they travel along or under the ground.

A *secondary shoot,* similar to the primary shoot, develops when a node roots and sprouts along a rhizome or stolon.

CLIMATE AND GRASS GROWTH

On page 9 is a map of the eight major lawn-growing areas in the United States and southern Canada. Lawns within an area share the same general temperatures, precipitation, topography, and soil type; however, a map like this reflects generalities only. Local variations, as well as your own pattern of lawn care, can outweigh these factors. (Don't confuse this map with the U.S. Department of Agriculture's Plant Hardiness Zone Map, which is based on temperature only.)

Grasses are categorized as either cool season or warm season. Warm-season grasses are best adapted to the southern part of the United States and other areas with hot summers and mild winters. They grow vigorously in the warm summer months and, depending on the variety and location, undergo winter dormancy, turning

Anatomy of a Grass Plant

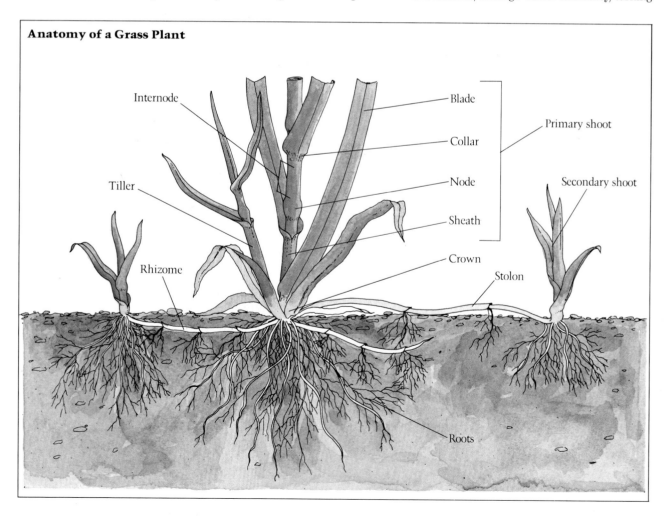

Internode
Blade
Collar
Primary shoot
Tiller
Node
Secondary shoot
Sheath
Rhizome
Crown
Stolon
Roots

Lawn Grass Climate Map

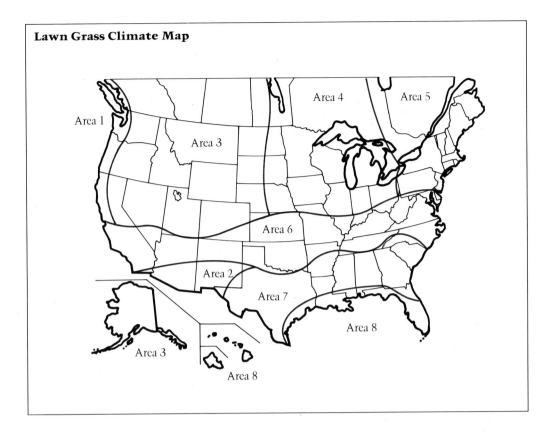

yellow or brown during the colder months. In milder climates, particularly in coastal areas, they may stay green all year. Warm-season grasses do not thrive in cold climates. Common warm-season grasses are bahiagrass, bermudagrass, centipedegrass, St. Augustine grass, and zoysiagrass. Buffalograss and blue grama, both North American natives, will tolerate somewhat colder climates than will other warm-season types.

Cool-season grasses grow well in the northern United States and other regions with warm summers and cold winters. They also perform well at high elevations and along the mild, dry coastal belts of California. They grow actively in the cool weather of spring and fall, and more slowly in summer heat. In snowy climates they go dormant during winter. Cool-season grasses do not thrive in intense summer heat, although they are often grown where summers are hot. Drought during the warmer months may cause them to go dormant, but with proper watering they will stay green throughout the growing season. Some commonly planted cool-season grasses include bentgrass, Kentucky bluegrass, fine fescues, turf-type tall fescue, and annual and perennial ryegrass.

In warm climates seeds of an annual cool-season grass such as annual ryegrass are often sown over a warm-season lawn during the winter months. This provides a temporary green cover while the warm-season grass lies dormant. With the onset of spring, the warm-season grass turns green again and the annual grass dies out.

If you live on a border between climate areas, you may have difficulty determining what area you are in. Ask your local nursery or agricultural extension service for advice.

Area 1—Cool and Humid

This is the Pacific Northwest, west of the Cascade range. Rainfall here is plentiful and soil is typically acid. There is marked seasonal change, although summers and winters are milder than those of other northern states. Lawns seeded from cool-season bentgrass, Kentucky bluegrass, fine fescues, and perennial ryegrass stay a beautiful green all year long. In fact, this area is the nation's center for cool-season grass seed production.

Area 2—Hot and Dry Summers

This area is the southernmost portion of the arid Southwest, where rainfall is low and temperatures are high. All lawns here need some supplemental watering. Soil is usually alkaline.

Lawns are primarily bermudagrass with some St. Augustine grass and zoysiagrass. Given adequate water, turf-type tall fescue can grow all year where the temperatures are not too hot. Perennial ryegrass is often used to overseed warm-season grasses that go dormant during winter. Buffalograss is sometimes used in northern parts of this area when a low-maintenance native grass is desired.

Area 3—Cold and Arid

This vast area stretches west from the Great Plains to the Sierra and Cascade ranges, north into Canada and Alaska, and south into Utah and Colorado. Much of the area is subject to drying winds and has relatively little rain; grasses here must endure wide temperature fluctuations. Cool-season Kentucky bluegrass and fine fescues predominate, but they generally require some extra watering. Turf-type tall fescues are becoming popular. Native grasses, such as buffalograss and wheatgrass, are often used where watering is difficult because of their drought tolerance and tenacity.

Area 4—Cold Winters and Summer Rains

The midwestern United States and central Canada make up this area. Soil is not as acid as in neighboring Area 5, and there is less rainfall. Summers are warm and humid. With the exception of a few zoysiagrass lawns in the southern portion of this area, cool-season grasses such as those grown in Area 5 predominate. Buffalograss is also grown.

Area 5—Cold and Humid

This area includes the northeastern United States and southeastern Canada. It is an area of abundant rainfall and acid soil. Summers are hot and humid, winters are cold and snowy. Cool-season bentgrass, Kentucky bluegrass, fine fescues, and perennial ryegrass predominate. Zoysiagrass is occasionally found in its southern portions along the Atlantic coast.

Area 6—Transition

In this transition belt across the entire United States, grass climates overlap, depending on many local factors. Both warm-season and cool-season grasses are common. It is critical to select the appropriate grass type, since neither cool-season nor warm-season grasses adapt

ideally in every part of this area. Turf-type tall fescue and zoysiagrass make good lawns in many areas of this region. Cold-tolerant cultivars of bermudagrass are also grown.

Area 7—Hot and Humid

Most lawns in this area, which includes Texas and the Deep South, consist of warm-season bermudagrass, centipedegrass, St. Augustine grass, and zoysiagrass. Kentucky bluegrass, fine fescues, turf-type tall fescue, and perennial ryegrass are grown in cooler parts of the area. Rainfall is high, summers are warm and humid, winters are fairly mild.

Area 8—Tropical

This area includes the Gulf Coast states, southern Florida, and much of Hawaii. It is a tropical climate; rainfall can be as high as 70 to 80 inches annually. Temperatures are relatively high throughout the year, and there is little or no frost. Too much water is as much a problem here as too little water can be in the Southwest. Bahiagrass, bermudagrass, centipedegrass, and St. Augustine grass make good lawns throughout this area. Zoysiagrass grows well in most parts of this area. Cool-season varieties such as bentgrass, fine fescues, and ryegrasses are used for overseeding dormant warm-season grasses in winter. Because of the longer growing season, all grasses in this area need more mowing and fertilizer than in colder regions.

A GALLERY OF GRASSES

This section describes the most commonly grown cool-season and warm-season grasses in the United States and southern Canada. Also described are native grasses, which are becoming popular because they tolerate drought and need little maintenance.

Each grass type is listed by its common name, followed by its botanical name. Most grasses are sold by their common name, with the botanical name listed along with it on the package. For example, the botanical name for Kentucky bluegrass is *Poa pratensis.* The first name, *Poa,* refers to the plant's genus, or group of related species—in this case, the bluegrasses. The second name, *pratensis,* refers to a species within the group—in this case, Kentucky bluegrass.

Within each description you will also see a listing of cultivars. A cultivar (short for *cultivated variety*) is a variation within a species. The term is often used interchangeably with *variety.* A cultivar may have special traits that make it superior to others for a given environment; check with your local nursery to determine which is best for you.

As you read the descriptions, note the recommendations regarding sowing and watering requirements, mowing height, fertilizer requirements, drought resistance, insect and disease susceptibility, and thatch development. This information is a clue to how much maintenance the grass will need. (For a quick overview of these traits, see the Lawn Grass Comparisons chart on page 21.)

Note that the suggested application rates for fertilizer are the optimum amounts for the season of active growth. Most lawns can get by on much less, however, even at the height of the growing season. "Actual nitrogen" refers to the weight of the nitrogen in the fertilizer product. For example, a 10-pound bag of 10 percent nitrogen fertilizer contains 1 pound of actual nitrogen. To determine how much fertilizer of a given formulation you need, see pages 70 and 71.

Cool-Season Grasses

There are three major types of cool-season grasses: bluegrasses, fescues, and ryegrasses. Bentgrass is another type, but it requires more maintenance and is not as adaptable as the others are to various climate zones; it is used primarily on golf greens and in the Pacific Northwest.

The blades of bluegrasses all have a characteristic boat-shaped tip, with the edges curved up like the sides of a canoe. Most are relatively cold tolerant but need generous amounts of water and fertilizer. Kentucky bluegrass is the most popular; rough bluegrass is often added to shade mixtures.

Fescues come in many forms and are generally classified as fine or coarse. The fine-textured fescues described here are chewings, hard, and red fescue. Turf-type tall fescue has coarser blades but better wear tolerance than the fine-textured fescues, and it does better in hotter areas.

Ryegrasses tend to clump rather than form runners, as many other grasses do. They germinate and establish themselves quickly, and are used in low-cost mixtures to cover large areas.

Creeping bentgrass

Creeping Bentgrass
Agrostis palustris
Creeping bentgrass is used extensively in cool climates for golf course putting greens and tees, lawn bowling greens, grass tennis courts, and some home lawns. It produces a fine-textured, soft, very dense, carpetlike lawn. However, it must be carefully tended or it can quickly lose its attractiveness.

To plant bentgrass from seed, sow ½ to 1 pound per 1,000 square feet; seed usually germinates within 4 to 12 days. The cultivars that grow best from seed include 'Emerald', 'Penncross', 'Penneagle', 'Pennlinks', 'Providence', and 'Seaside'. Bentgrass can also be started from sprigs, using 2 bushels per 1,000 square feet. Sod is available but very expensive.

Bentgrass needs frequent watering (almost daily on golf courses; up to three times a week on home lawns, depending on the weather). It is tolerant of acid soils and somewhat tolerant of shade. It requires low mowing (¼ to ¾ inches high).

Its fertilizer requirements are high. For highest quality, use ½ to 1 pound of actual nitrogen per 1,000 square feet per month of active growth; for medium quality, use half that amount per growing month.

The extensive production of stolons can quickly result in a thick mat of thatch, which needs to be removed on a regular basis in a procedure known as dethatching (see pages 76 and 77). If this is not done, the thatch layer can become quite thick, preventing water and nutrients from reaching the soil. A simple way to slow the buildup of thatch is to reduce the amount of fertilizer bentgrass receives. This will also retard its growth rate, reducing the need for frequent watering and mowing. But because the lawn is growing less vigorously, diseases and weeds will be somewhat more of a problem; keep an eye out for these. (See the fourth chapter.)

Even when fertilized optimally (and therefore growing vigorously), creeping bentgrass is susceptible to a wide range of diseases, including brown patch, dollar spot, fusarium patch, red thread, summer patch, and typhula blight.

Good cultivars include 'Penncross', which is dense, disease resistant, and quick to recover from damage; 'Providence', which is darker green and has more of an upright growth habit; and 'Seaside', which tends to develop less thatch than some others. Other good cultivars are 'Cobra', 'Emerald', 'Penneagle', 'Pennlinks', 'Prominent', and 'Putter'.

Kentucky Bluegrass
Poa pratensis

Kentucky bluegrass is the most widely planted cool-season grass, especially in the northern latitudes. Blue-green in color, medium to fine textured, and very cold hardy, it represents the standard for appearance against which other cool-season grasses are measured. It is widely used for lawns, athletic fields, golf fairways, and general-purpose turfs because of its beauty. Even so, it requires conscientious maintenance.

It is best adapted in northern states east of the Rockies, in the Pacific Northwest, and at higher elevations in the South.

When planting Kentucky bluegrass from seed, use 1 to 2 pounds per 1,000 square feet. Since it germinates rather slowly (14 to 30 days), seed of faster-sprouting grasses is often mixed in. Kentucky bluegrass is often sold as sod because its strong underground rhizomes and aboveground tillers weave a dense mat that holds together for easy transporting and installing.

Mow it to between 1½ and 2½ inches high, slightly higher during hot weather to shade the sensitive crown area.

Kentucky bluegrass thrives best with frequent watering and generous fertilizing (½ to 1 pound of actual nitrogen per 1,000 square feet per month of active growth), but it can cope with some deprivation. If lawn watering is restricted, Kentucky bluegrass will survive drought periods by going dormant.

Kentucky bluegrass is susceptible to several diseases, including dollar spot, leaf spot, rust, stripe smut, and summer patch—and is thus considered fairly disease prone. However, some newer cultivars offer improved disease resistance.

Among the most useful cultivars is 'Adelphi', which is low growing, dark green, and fine leafed; it is especially disease resistant, fairly tolerant of shade and heat, and attractive even under low maintenance. 'Eclipse', a newer cultivar, tolerates shade and resists most diseases; low growing, medium textured, and dark green, it establishes itself quickly and grows densely and vigorously.

Rough Bluegrass
Poa trivialis

A bright green, fine-textured, and shallow-rooted grass with boat-shaped tips to its blades, this relative of Kentucky bluegrass is noted for its high tolerance of moist soils and shade. The grass is soft, cold hardy, and retains its color over winter in mild climates. It makes a good component in shady-lawn mixtures, but in sunny areas it tends to crowd out other worthwhile grasses, particularly Kentucky bluegrass and perennial ryegrass. Most rough bluegrass is grown in the same locations as is Kentucky bluegrass.

To establish a permanent lawn in cool-season areas, sow 2 pounds of seed per 1,000 square feet in sunshine; use 3 pounds per 1,000 square feet in shade. Rough bluegrass germinates fairly

Kentucky bluegrass

Rough bluegrass

Chewings fescue

slowly (14 to 30 days). It is sometimes mixed (10 to 15 percent) with perennial ryegrass for winter overseeding in the South. When used for overseeding, as much as 15 to 20 pounds of this mixture is applied per 1,000 square feet.

Needing ample amounts of water, rough bluegrass does not tolerate drought well because of its shallow root system, nor does it wear well under traffic. In sunny areas that become dry, permanent lawns of rough bluegrass can thin out and turn brown, so it is important to keep the soil moist. If this is impossible, choose another variety of grass.

Its growth habit is prostrate with slender, creeping stolons. Lacking rhizomes to bind it together, it does not form the tight, vigorous sod that Kentucky bluegrass does. This also makes it less tolerant of wear.

Ideal mowing height is 1½ to 2 inches. Fertilizer needs are moderate; between ¼ to ½ pound of actual nitrogen should be applied per 1,000 square feet during each growing month.

Diseases that cause occasional problems include brown patch, fusarium patch, rust, stripe smut, and typhula blight.

Popular cultivars are 'Colt', 'Laser', and 'Sabre'. The last has a darker green color and grows lower and slightly more densely than the other two; it can survive well in wet, shady situations. None of these cultivars are able to thrive in heat and drought.

Fine Fescues
Festuca species and varieties

Fine fescues, including chewings, hard, and red fescue, are very fine leafed grasses that are used extensively in seed blends for both sunny and shady situations. They germinate rapidly (7 to 14 days) and establish themselves quickly. They are medium green in color and spread by tillers or short creeping rhizomes. During

extended hot, dry periods, fine fescues may lose their color rapidly.

Chewings fescue (*Festuca rubra commutata*) is an aggressive, bunch-type fine fescue that can overtake other grasses—a bad quality if you want to preserve these but good if you want to crowd out weeds. Because of its high shade tolerance, it is sometimes used to overseed shady lawns, often in mixtures with perennial ryegrass. Its lack of rhizomes gives it a noncreeping growth habit and only moderate wear tolerance. It forms more thatch than other fine fescues.

Chewings fescue is best adapted to cooler areas in the northern United States and Canada, the coastal regions of the Northeast and Pacific Northwest, and elsewhere where summers are cool. It is well adapted to the sandy, acidic, often infertile soils that are found in these regions. It is sometimes included with Kentucky bluegrass in cool-season mixes.

When planting a lawn of chewings fescue from seed, use about 5 pounds per 1,000 square feet. It germinates in 7 to 10 days. Keep it mowed to 1 to 2½ inches high. Its fertilizer needs are moderate. During its active growing period, apply ¼ to ½ pound of actual nitrogen per 1,000 square feet per month.

One weakness of this species is its susceptibility to fungal disease when the weather is hot and wet. Another is its inability to wear well under traffic. It is slow to reestablish after the roots have been damaged.

Popular cultivars include 'Banner', which is better suited to coastal areas, and 'Shadow', which is noted for its adaptation to shade and moderately good resistance to diseases. Others include 'Highlight', 'Jamestown', 'Mary', and 'Victory'. 'Jamestown II', an improved cultivar, contains a genetically transferred fungus that makes it distasteful to surface-feeding insects.

Hard fescue

Red fescue

Hard fescue (*Festuca ovina* var. *duriuscula*) is a fine-textured grass found mostly in the northern United States and Canada and at high elevations. Growing in clumps, it is slower to fill in and become established than chewings and red fescue, but it needs minimal maintenance when mature. It has thin, firm leaves and does not form rhizomes, making it somewhat less resistant to wear.

Hard fescue is tolerant of shade in well-drained soils and is fairly drought resistant and salt tolerant. Highly resistant to diseases such as dollar spot, leaf spot, and red thread, it is generally healthier than other fine fescues. It also stays greener over summer, even during extended dry periods. Its wearability is fair, though the clumps do recover slowly from damage. Although newer cultivars have been improved, some hard fescues are difficult to mow evenly, leaving the blade tips shredded and discolored.

Hard fescue is most often sold as seed. Although it can be purchased straight, it is more often included in grass seed mixtures with bluegrasses, perennial ryegrasses, and other fine fescues, increasing their adaptability and vigor. If sowing it straight, apply 3½ to 4½ pounds per 1,000 square feet. Seeds germinate in 7 to 14 days.

Mow hard fescue at 1 to 2½ inches. Its fertilizer needs are a moderate ¼ to ½ pound of actual nitrogen per 1,000 square feet per growing month.

Among common cultivars, 'Aurora' is disease resistant and well adapted to shade. Other shade lovers include 'Biljart', 'Reliant', 'Spartan', and 'Waldina'. 'Reliant' is also noted for its ability to thrive under low-maintenance conditions. All of these cultivars mow evenly. The cultivar 'SR-3000' contains an internal fungus organism that makes it unpalatable to surface-feeding insects.

Red fescue (*Festuca rubra*), also called creeping red fescue, is a frequent component of bluegrass mixtures. A fine-textured grass with narrow, dark green blades, it blends well and does what some bluegrasses cannot—it grows well in both shade and drought. Red fescue is preferable to chewings fescue in a seed mixture because it is more heat tolerant and less likely to form thatch.

It is best adapted where summers are cool, such as in the coastal Northwest and at high elevations. It is widely planted in the Great Lakes region.

Growing well on banks and slopes, it creates an especially lush effect when left unmowed. It is also good for overseeding dormant warm-season grasses in winter, provided that it is spared a lot of foot traffic. It has a creeping growth habit, spreading by rhizomes and tillers.

It is usually seeded at the rate of 2 to 4 pounds per 1,000 square feet, and germinates in 7 to 14 days. It is normally mowed at 1½ to 2½ inches, but it may be left unmowed to create a meadow effect. Its fertilizer needs are a moderate ¼ to ½ pound of actual nitrogen per 1,000 square feet per growing month.

When grown in hot climates, red fescue is very susceptible to summer diseases, especially in moist, fertile soil. It tends to thin and turn brownish in hot, dry weather. It tolerates acid soil but is slow to recover from wear and damage. Red fescue does not tolerate wet soils or excess nitrogen.

Dollar spot, fusarium patch, powdery mildew, red thread, and typhula blight are diseases that can damage red fescue.

Cultivars include 'Dawson', with a medium green color and good shade tolerance; 'Pennlawn', a fast spreader that can be mowed low; and 'Boreal', 'Fortress', 'Ruby', and 'Shademaster'—all good for shade.

Tall Fescue
Festuca arundinacea
A dense clumping grass that forms a coarse turf able to grow in sun or shade, this species stays green all year in mild-winter climates. It is a good general grass for home lawns as well as for playing fields and commercial grounds. Its disadvantages are its coarse texture and clumping style of growth. It does best in areas of mild winters and warm summers, and in mild-temperature regions of the Southwest.

Seed sown at a rate of 6 to 10 pounds per 1,000 square feet germinates in 7 to 12 days. Seedlings are vigorous and fast growing. Turf-type tall fescues and turf-type dwarf fescues are also available as sod in some areas. The latter, a subcategory of the taller kind, is new on the market. Cultivars of this grass grow more densely than the nondwarf varieties, are quite drought resistant, and require less mowing because they do not grow as rapidly.

Mow tall fescues to 2 to 3 inches for home lawns or 1½ to 2 inches for athletic use. Dwarf fescue should be mowed to 1½ to 2½ inches. Both have moderate fertilizer needs; depending on the amount of wear the lawn receives, use ¼ to ½ pound of actual nitrogen per 1,000 square feet per growing month.

Tall fescue is tolerant of warm temperatures and wear. Its dense root system, penetrating as deep as 4 feet, makes it one of the most drought resistant of cool-season grasses. It maintains its color in cool, but not severe, winter conditions.

Older varieties, such as 'Kentucky 31' or 'Alta', are coarse textured, while the newer types have more medium-textured leaves and denser tillering. The latter quality enables turf-type tall fescue to fill in open spacing more quickly. Newer types, including 'Apache', 'Arid', and 'Mustang', offer improved shade tolerance and resistance to insects, and require less water and fertilizer. They also wear well.

Tall fescue

Solid stands of tall fescue may thin out after several years. Overseeding with additional tall fescue seeds at approximately 3 to 5 pounds per 1,000 square feet will help correct this problem. Both tall and dwarf fescue often appear as clumping, annoying weeds in finer cool-season lawns. They can be dug out or spot treated with glyphosate (see page 109).

Tall and dwarf fescue are susceptible to the brown patch, fusarium patch, and typhula blight diseases.

Best cultivars are 'Adventure', which tolerates both full sun and partial shade well, and 'Jaguar II', which is noted for its fall color retention and tolerance of heat, drought, and shade. Others are 'Mustang' (good for shade) and the lower-growing dwarf varieties 'Arid', 'El Camino Dwarf', 'Hubbard 87', 'Medallion Dwarf', 'Mustang', and 'Rebel Jr.'

Annual Ryegrass, Italian Ryegrass
Lolium multiflorum
Annual ryegrass is a cool-season annual or, in cooler climates, a short-lived perennial bunch-type grass. It forms a medium- to coarse-textured lawn with moderate wear resistance. In temperate climates, it is sometimes used as a temporary lawn in late spring. In mild-winter areas of the southern, southwestern, and Pacific states, it is often used to overseed dormant warm-season grasses for winter color.

Planted by seed at the rate of 5 to 10 pounds per 1,000 square feet, it germinates rapidly (5 to 10 days) and is quick to establish itself. It is mowed 1½ to 2 inches high and fertilized moderately (¼ to ½ pound of actual nitrogen per 1,000 square feet per growing month).

Annual ryegrass, Italian ryegrass

Perennial ryegrass

The blades of annual ryegrass are lighter green and coarser in texture than those of perennial ryegrass. Its growth habit is upright and bunching, with no rhizomes or stolons.

Best grown in full sun, this grass requires a moderate to large amount of water and is not drought tolerant. It also has poor tolerance of heat and cold. Moreover, its clumping growth pattern makes for an uneven surface that is difficult to mow cleanly. Because its aggressive growth tends to crowd out more desirable cool-season grasses, it is not used in seed mixtures.

Cultivars include 'Agree' and 'Oregon', both hybrids of a cross between annual ryegrass and perennial ryegrass.

Perennial Ryegrass
Lolium perenne
Deep green glossy leaf blades, a shallow root system, and a texture that is finer than annual ryegrass characterize this grass. Exhibiting the best wear tolerance of any cool-season grass, it is often used as a tough play lawn. However, its intolerance of extreme heat, cold, and drought make it best adapted to coastal regions with mild winters and cool, moist summers. In southern states, it is sometimes used instead of annual ryegrass to overseed dormant lawns of warm-season bermudagrass during winter. But unlike annual ryegrass, it tends to persist during the transition from cool to warm weather—

a disadvantage if you want the bermudagrass to predominate again when summer returns.

Perennial ryegrass likes full sun but will tolerate some shade. Its noncreeping, bunch-type growth forms a uniform lawn if the grass is properly established and maintained.

Perennial ryegrass can be planted as either seed or sod. When planting seed, sow 5 to 10 pounds per 1,000 square feet. It germinates in 5 to 10 days. It combines especially well with Kentucky bluegrass and fine fescues.

Its fertilizer needs are moderate (¼ to ½ pound of actual nitrogen per 1,000 square feet per growing month). If you grow this grass in a play area, use the higher amount of fertilizer. Ideal mowing height is 1½ to 2 inches.

Fusarium patch, pythium blight, red thread, rust, stripe smut, and typhula blight are diseases that can harm perennial ryegrass.

The cultivar 'Birdie II' is one of the best perennial ryegrasses for overseeding bermudagrass. Unlike older cultivars, it is relatively shade tolerant. Additional cultivars that can grow successfully in shade include 'Cowboy', 'Gator', 'Palmer', 'Pennant', 'Yorktown II', and 'Prelude', which also tolerates heat, cold, drought, and close mowing. The cultivars 'All Star', 'Citation II', 'Jazz', 'Repell', 'Saturn', 'SR-4000', and 'SR-4100' are resistant to surface-feeding insects.

Warm-Season Grasses
Unlike cool-season grasses, warm-season grasses grow vigorously during hot weather and go dormant during cool or cold winters. With adequate nitrogen fertilizer, these grasses may stay green all year in very mild climates. If their winter brownness is displeasing, they can be overseeded with a cool-season grass such as annual ryegrass. Even in their winter brown or straw-colored state, warm-season grasses can help keep mud from being tracked into the house.

Bahiagrass, hybrid bermudagrass, and St. Augustine grass send out runners that fill in a lawn quickly. Centipedegrass and zoysiagrass are slower to cover. Once established, any of these will usually crowd out most broadleaf weeds. The hybrid bermudagrasses need frequent mowing and dethatching.

Most warm-season grasses are vigorous growers that tend to be invasive. Some type of edging is normally installed to contain them.

Bahiagrass

Paspalum notatum

Bahiagrass is a tough, coarse-textured, moderately aggressive grass that is adapted to a wide range of soil conditions. It is grown from the central coast of North Carolina to eastern Texas. It is also found in central and southwestern Florida.

Planted from sod or from seed (at a rate of 8 to 10 pounds of seed per 1,000 square feet), it spreads by short rhizomes and grows best in sandy, slightly acid, infertile soil, in either full sun or partial shade. Its extensive root system makes it valuable for erosion control and a good grass for drought-prone areas. However, it does best where rainfall is regular and plentiful. It is especially suited to roadsides, airfields, and other expanses requiring a minimum-quality, minimum-maintenance grass.

Because it develops tall, fast-growing seed stalks, bahiagrass is considered a weed when it occurs in lawns of other warm-season grasses. A bahiagrass lawn thus needs frequent mowing (2 to 3 inches high) to keep it looking attractive. Brown patch and dollar spot diseases and mole crickets can be troublesome. Fertilizer needs are low; use ¼ to ½ pound of actual nitrogen per 1,000 square feet per growing month.

The cultivar 'Argentine' is used most often for lawns because of its dense growth, attractive shade of green, and disease resistance.

Common Bermudagrass

Cynodon dactylon

A fine- to medium-textured grass that spreads and fills in quickly by rhizomes and stolons, common bermudagrass has deep roots that help make it tolerant of heat and drought (although it looks better if given adequate water).

Easily grown in most soils, it resists many diseases and can take considerable wear and abuse. These qualities make it popular for lawns, sports fields, and roadsides.

Common bermudagrass is best adapted to lower elevations of the Southwest and the region bounded by Maryland, Florida, Texas, and Kansas. It is also grown in mild-winter areas along the West Coast.

Invasive by nature, common bermudagrass can be hard to keep out of areas where it is not wanted. Its vigorous growth rate also makes it prone to form thatch. It does not grow well in shade, and it often goes dormant when fall temperatures drop below 50° or 60° F, turning yellow or brown until spring.

In humid areas, common bermudagrass is susceptible to diseases such as brown patch, dollar spot, leaf spot, and pythium blight, and to pests such as armyworms, bermudagrass mites, nematodes, and sod webworms.

Plant it from seed at a rate of 1 to 2 pounds per 1,000 square feet; seeds germinate in 10 to 30 days. Fertilizer needs are high—½ to 1 pound of actual nitrogen per 1,000 square feet per growing month. Common bermudagrass needs to be mowed often, to a height of ¾ to 1½ inches, cutting off ½ inch or less each time. Use a reel or rotary mower.

Good cultivars are 'Arizona' and 'U-3'.

Hybrid Bermudagrass

Cynodon species

Softer, denser, and finer textured than common bermudagrass, hybrid bermudagrass is a fast-growing, durable, heat-loving grass used for home lawns and golf courses. It is considered fairly drought tolerant, but like common bermudagrass, it looks better if given more

Bahiagrass

Common bermudagrass

'Tifway' hybrid bermudagrass

Centipedegrass

water. It also needs more frequent mowing (twice a week during active growth periods), somewhat more fertilizer, and full sun.

It is popular in the South, Southwest, Southeast, and mild-winter areas along the West Coast.

Seed of hybrid bermudagrass is sterile; thus sod, sprigs, or plugs are used for propagation. If you plant sprigs, spread 2 bushels per 1,000 square feet. Alternatively, plant 2-inch plugs 12 inches apart.

Mow to ½ to 1 inch, cutting off less than ½ inch at each mowing. A reel mower rather than a rotary mower should be used because it can cut that low more easily, and because it gives the lawn a more manicured appearance. The lawn will tend to yellow if it is allowed to grow longer. The root system can be invasive, and regular thatch control may be required. Hybrid bermudagrass is a heavy feeder—use ¾ to 1 pound of actual nitrogen per 1,000 square feet per growing month. However, it is freer of diseases and pests than common bermudagrass.

Widely used cultivars of hybrid bermudagrass are 'Tifway', which needs less maintenance than others and is one of the best for home lawns; 'Santa Ana', noted for its tolerance to wear, salt, and smog, and its color retention in cold weather; and 'Tifgreen', often used on golf greens.

Centipedegrass
Eremochloa ophiuroides
Centipedegrass is a coarse-textured, light green grass that creeps low to the ground by way of leafy stolons. It is grown primarily in the Southeast and in Hawaii. It adapts to poor soil, resists chinch bugs and brown patch disease, and is aggressive enough to crowd out weeds. It also requires less mowing than other grasses. These qualities and its slow growth make it an excellent low-maintenance, general-purpose lawn.

Centipedegrass has some drawbacks, however. Because of its shallow roots, it has only moderate drought tolerance and is among the first of the warm-season grasses to turn brown during extended hot, dry periods. Also sensitive to low temperatures, it tends to turn brown and go dormant when cold. It turns green again when temperatures warm up. It will not withstand much traffic and is slow to recover when damaged. It should not be planted near beach areas, since it cannot tolerate salt spray.

To plant, sow 1 to 2 pounds of 'Centiseed' (the only cultivar of centipedegrass that can be grown from seed) per 1,000 square feet. Seeds germinate in about 20 days but are slow to fill in and establish a dense lawn. Other cultivars must be planted from sprigs, plugs, or sod. If using sprigs, plant 5 to 6 bushels per 1,000 square feet, placing the sprigs 9 to 12 inches apart. If planting plugs, set 2-inch plugs 6 inches apart. Centipedegrass prefers full sun but tolerates some shade.

Centipedegrass requires very little fertilizer—just ¹⁄₁₀ to ³⁄₁₀ pound per 1,000 square feet per growing month. If yellowing occurs, the cause is probably chlorosis, an iron or manganese deficiency that often afflicts warm-season grasses during cool spring weather, when their uptake of nutrients is less efficient. You may need to apply chelated iron at 0.05 to 0.07 pounds per 1,000 square feet; or ferrous sulfate at 0.1 to 0.15 pounds per 1,000 square feet. (Either one works well.) Use the greater amounts if yellowing is severe. The ideal mowing height is 1 to 2 inches.

Brown patch and dollar spot diseases, ground pearls, and nematodes can do damage to centipedegrass.

The cultivars 'Centennial' and 'Oaklawn' are best established from sprigs rather than sod. 'Oaklawn' has better drought and cold tolerance than some other cultivars.

St. Augustine Grass
Stenotaphrum secundatum

A robust and fast-growing coarse-textured grass with broad, dark green blades, St. Augustine grass is among the most shade tolerant of the warm-season grasses. It spreads aggressively by stolons and crowds out most weeds. Best adapted to southern California, Hawaii, mild areas of the Southwest, and Florida and other Gulf Coast states, it is tolerant of salt sprays and salty soil. It also tolerates heat. On the minus side, it requires frequent watering and tends to lose its color under cold conditions.

Plant St. Augustine grass from 3- or 4-inch sod plugs, spaced 1 foot apart. Mow at 1½ to 2½ inches. Mowing height is critical to the appearance of this grass. If it is mowed too low, weeds are more likely to gain a foothold. If it is mowed too high, heavy thatch can build up quickly.

Fertilizer needs are moderate—use ½ to 1 pound of actual nitrogen per 1,000 square feet per growing month. This grass responds well to applications of ferrous sulfate or chelated iron. These compounds enhance the appearance of St. Augustine grass and help prevent yellowing from chlorosis.

Chinch bugs, mole crickets, and sod webworms can do considerable damage during the warmer months. During cooler weather, when the grass turns partially brown and becomes semidormant, brown patch disease can be a problem. Some varieties are susceptible to St. Augustine grass decline (SAD) virus.

Cultivars include 'Seville', which resists SAD virus and stays green longer in colder weather; 'Tamlawn', which resists SAD and gray leaf spot; and 'Floratine', which is particularly tolerant of shade.

Zoysiagrass
Zoysia species

Tolerant of heat and drought, yet able to endure some shade, zoysiagrass forms a dense, wiry, fine-textured lawn that crowds out weeds. However, the needlelike blades of many varieties can be sharp underfoot. Zoysiagrass grows best in coastal areas of the South and throughout southern California.

St. Augustine grass

Zoysiagrass

Plant it from sod or from 2-inch plugs spaced 6 inches apart. It is a slow grower, sometimes requiring two full growing seasons to become established from its creeping rhizomes and stolons.

Zoysiagrass should be mowed 1 to 2 inches high. If left too long, the wiry blades are tough to mow. Its fertilizer needs are a modest ¼ to ½ pound of actual nitrogen per 1,000 square feet per growing month. Too much nitrogen promotes thatch buildup, so it is important not to exceed the recommended amount.

It is relatively untroubled by diseases and pests; however, brown patch and dollar spot are potential diseases, and armyworms, billbugs, and sod webworms can cause problems.

Zoysiagrass does not thrive where summers are short or cool. It goes dormant sooner in winter than other warm-season grasses and may stay brown longer.

Cultivars of zoysiagrass include 'Meyer', which tolerates low temperatures, drought, and wear, but not shade; and 'El Toro' and 'Emerald', which can stand partial shade better than most. The cultivars 'Meyer' and 'Emerald' have relatively soft blades that are easier on bare feet.

Blue grama

Smooth brome

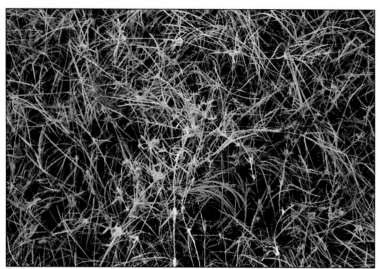
Buffalograss

Native Grasses

Several of the world's thousands of native grasses make excellent ground covers. Their minimal needs for water and fertilizer, their tolerance of a wide temperature range, their resistance to pests and diseases, and their infrequent need for mowing—just three or four times a year for some, and less often for others—has made them increasingly popular. Often planted on hillsides, along roadways, and in other neglected spots, they help control wind and water erosion to stabilize the soil.

Because they have not been bred for uniformity, they do not make the most attractive home lawns. Moreover, many turn brown at the end of their growing season and some are annuals that must be replanted each year if they fail to reseed themselves. However, they offer variations in color and height that add a natural, informal look to a landscape.

These grasses generally need only two fertilizer applications a year to keep them healthy. Apply a complete fertilizer such as 10-5-5 or 12-6-4 in midspring and early fall.

Blue Grama
Bouteloua gracilis

Grayish green and fine textured, blue grama exhibits excellent tolerance of heat, cold, drought, and alkaline soil. An important native of the Great Plains, it is used in rangeland settings or in similar, rarely watered situations. Although technically a warm-season grass, it remains hardy to -40° F. Blue grama seed is often mixed with buffalograss seed for a better-looking ground cover.

To plant, use 1 to 3 pounds of seed per 1,000 square feet. Because blue grama is slow to germinate and become established, seed should be sown in early spring or during the previous fall to give it a long head start. Allow about 30 days for germination. Mow to 2 or 3 inches.

Buffalograss
Buchloe dactyloides

One of the dominant grasses of the American prairie, buffalograss has fine-textured blades with outstanding heat tolerance. Gray-green from late spring to hard frost, this warm-season grass turns straw colored through the dormant period of late fall and winter. It does well in heavy soil.

Often used as a low-maintenance, drought-tolerant lawn, buffalograss thrives in areas that receive 12 to 25 inches of rain per year. This includes the area from Minnesota to central Montana, and south from Minnesota to Iowa, Texas, Arizona, and northern Mexico.

Buffalograss is easily started from seed sown at the rate of 2 pounds per 1,000 square feet; it should germinate in 14 to 21 days. Slow to fill in (it takes about two seasons to fill a planting area), buffalograss spreads rapidly by surface runners once established. Because these runners can invade surrounding flower beds, it is a good idea to install an edging such as the ones described on page 31. Buffalograss can also be established by planting 2-inch plugs at 1-foot intervals, no earlier than April 15 in cold-winter areas, or as soon as the soil warms in mild-winter areas. Plugs spread quickly, filling the lawn within the first growing season. Water to a depth of 1 foot until the grass is established; then little water is needed. To start from sod in spring, plant 4-inch plugs 3 to 4 feet apart in prepared soil.

Buffalograss makes a matted, reasonably dense turf that takes hard wear and looks fairly good with very little summer watering. More lawnlike in character than other native grasses, it is becoming increasingly popular in drought-prone regions. Given minimal watering it grows to 4 inches tall and requires little or no mowing. More water promotes higher growth and the need for some mowing, usually at 2½ to 3 inches.

Improved varieties include 'Prairie', '609', and 'Texoka'.

Smooth Brome
Bromus inermis 'Leyss'
This cool-season native grass spreads aggressively by means of underground rhizomes. It can be grown in lawns and waysides and in pastures for forage. It can help restore eroded slopes. It prefers some moisture, but it will survive drought.

Smooth brome can be grown throughout most of the United States. However, it does not do well in southern regions with long periods of high humidity.

This grass is medium green, with ½-inch wide leaf blades that somewhat resemble St. Augustine grass. It turns a sour-apple green when temperatures drop in winter. Mow it to 3 inches for residential areas, 6 inches in more rustic locations.

Lawn Grass Comparisons

	Establishment Speed	Heat Tolerance	Cold Tolerance	Drought Tolerance	Shade Tolerance	Wearability	Tolerance of Low Mowing	Fertilizer Economy
Cool-Season Grasses								
Creeping bentgrass	◐	◐	●	○	◐	◐	●	○
Kentucky bluegrass	○	◐	●	◐	◐	◐	◐	◐
Rough bluegrass	◐	○	●	○	●	◐	◐	◐
Fine fescues	◐	◐	●	◐	●	◐	◐	●
Tall fescue	◐	◐	◐	●	●	●	○	◐
Annual ryegrass	●	○	○	○	○	◐	○	◐
Perennial ryegrass	●	◐	◐	◐	◐	●	◐	◐
Warm-Season Grasses								
Bahiagrass	◐	●	○	◐	◐	●	○	●
Common bermudagrass	●	●	◐	●	○	●	●	◐
Hybrid bermudagrass	●	●	◐	●	○	●	●	◐
Centipedegrass	◐	●	○	◐	◐	○	◐	◐
St. Augustine grass	◐	●	○	○	●	◐	○	◐
Zoysiagrass	○	●	◐	●	◐	●	●	●

● = Good
◐ = Moderate
○ = Poor
Note: These are typical characteristics for each grass type. The performance of individual cultivars may vary.

Installing a Lawn

With the goal of a lush, green lawn in mind, you may be tempted to hurry through the initial steps of installing it. Avoid the temptation. Careful groundwork at this early stage is critical to your success.

There are a number of situations in which you may want to plant a new lawn. You may have built a new house and need to fill its bare grounds quickly. You may have added onto your home or constructed a pool or gazebo; the disruption caused by building may have damaged your lawn beyond repair.

You may wish to replace an existing lawn that has failed you in some way. It may have been destroyed by drought or pests, have become hopelessly encrusted with thatch, or be inadequate for your current needs. The procedures for this type of major renovation are described on pages 108 and 109.

The design of your lawn, the way you prepare for it, and the type of grass you select all have long-term implications. Answers to such questions as How will I use my lawn? Which grass should I plant? Do I want to sow seed or use sprigs, plugs, or sod? and How will I water? all should be fully thought out in advance of any labor. Read this chapter and look through the rest of the book before beginning work on your lawn; some forethought will save you many future headaches.

A sod lawn provides instant landscaping around a new home.

A lawn need not be strictly rectangular. Here, a zigzag border of white gravel (kept in line by wooden edging) creates a striking buffer zone between a lawn and its surrounding greenery.

DESIGNING A LAWN

The lawn and plantings you install today will be with you for years to come. When fitting a lawn into your landscape, think about the practical things—how you plan to use your yard and how easy it should be to maintain. Also think about aesthetics—how your lawn will complement nearby plantings and architecture, and how it will fit into the neighborhood.

As you plan, consider the natural environment in which your lawn will grow. Think about the soil, the amount of rainfall, any drainage problems you may have, the amount of shade, and the year-round climate.

Before you begin any work on your lawn, make as accurate a drawing of it as possible. Using graph paper, draw to scale everything you want in your yard, including paths, driveways, decks, patios, trees, and planting areas. It is important to take accurate measurements. These will help you plan an irrigation system, determine the quantities of soil amendments to buy, and estimate the amount of seed, sod, sprigs, or plugs you will need.

You may wish to hire a landscape designer or landscape contractor to draw up a set of accurate plans for you, including an irrigation design if desired. At the same time, this professional can advise you on the best type of grass to plant, and the types and amounts of materials you will need to install your lawn properly.

Marking the Lawn Area

Once you have completed your landscape plan, the next step is to mark off the lawn area on the ground. One method of marking the ground is to use landscape-marking paint, a special spray paint that can be purchased at many hardware and irrigation supply stores. Use different colors to mark the paths of irrigation and drainage lines you plan to bury in the ground.

Another method of marking boundaries is to use gypsum or lime—white powdered materials that are commonly used to adjust soil texture or pH. Dispense the powder along the ground by hand or from a large coffee can with several holes punched at a spot near the bottom. Holding the can close to the ground, shake the powder through the holes as you walk along.

Work should begin as soon as possible after the marking material has been applied, as it will remain clearly visible for only a day or two.

PREPARING FOR A LAWN

All lawns—whether planted from seed, sod, sprigs, or plugs—need rich, loose, weed-free soil in order to thrive. If you do not provide this at the start, your lawn will fail to reach its optimum level of appearance—if it survives at all.

Once you have designed your lawn and marked its rough boundaries, it is time to prepare the soil for planting. In most areas of the country, fall is the best time to plant a cool-season grass because the cooler weather favors its growth; however, any other time when temperatures are not extreme is also appropriate. Warm-season grasses are best planted in spring and early summer.

The amount of work you will have to do at this stage depends on the kind of soil you are starting with. If you are fortunate enough to have a loam soil with a proper grade, you may need to do little beyond thorough rotary tilling, fertilizing, and raking. Usually, though, more work is required. The following are the steps a professional landscaper takes to prepare the soil for a lawn.

Step 1: Evaluating the Soil

Much of the success of your lawn depends on how you prepare the soil. Remember that, unlike a vegetable garden where the soil can be amended or reworked each year, grass roots grow in the same soil year after year. Although most nutrient deficiencies can be corrected after the lawn has been established, changing the soil texture under growing grass is difficult and expensive. The effort you put into preparing the soil will be reflected in the health and beauty of your lawn for years to come. This is true for lawns planted with seed, sprigs, plugs, or sod. Even though sod has a small amount of soil already attached, proper site preparation is still critical to its success.

Soil texture   Gardeners use many terms to describe the texture of the soil in their area, including heavy, light, poor, lean, sandy, clay, and loam. Although these terms convey useful information about the quality of a soil, they tend to be imprecise. Scientists and horticulturists classify soil by the proportion of sand, silt, and clay it contains. These three classifications are based on the size of the individual soil particles—clay being the smallest, silt somewhat larger, and sand the largest. Soil texture is determined by the proportions of each of these various particles.

For proper growth, lawns need air in the soil, sufficient moisture (but not standing water), and a supply of mineral nutrients, such as nitrogen, phosphorus, potassium, and iron. If soil has plenty of clay, holding onto nutrients is no problem, but the small clay particles cling together so closely that they hold water and leave little room for air. When clay soil is

packed down under a lawn, water penetrates slowly to lawn roots. If it drains too slowly, the lawn may die. Clay soil is usually hard when dry and sticky when wet.

At the other extreme, sandy soil has plenty of room for air, but moisture and nutrients disappear quickly. Water sinks into sandy soil without moving laterally very much and dries up in just a few days after watering. If a handful of sandy soil is compressed, it quickly falls apart when it is released.

In between a sandy soil and a clay soil is a loam soil, the one best for lawn growth. Containing a combination of clay, silt, and sand, it retains nutrients and water while allowing sufficient room for air.

Chances are your soil is not the perfect loam, in which case it would benefit from the addition of organic matter such as compost or manure. Even if it is an ideal soil, heavy foot traffic or perhaps construction activity around new homes can severely compact it, closing air spaces and restricting water and nutrient penetration. You have seen the effects of compaction in footpaths worn across a lawn.

Soil pH   Along with texture, the acidity or alkalinity of the soil is important to the growth of lawn grasses, since excess acidity or alkalinity can make nutrients in the soil chemically inaccessible to plants. Before planting a lawn, you may need to adjust the pH of your soil so that grass can readily grow there.

The term pH refers to the relative acidity or alkalinity of a soil, which is measured on a scale of 0 to 14. Lower numbers indicate more acidic conditions and higher numbers more alkaline conditions. A pH of 7.0 is neutral—neither acidic nor alkaline.

The ideal pH for lawn grasses is 6.5 to 7.0, but most will flourish in the 5.5 to 7.5 range. In this range the important nutrients—nitrogen, phosphorus, and potassium—are most readily available to plant roots.

Soil pH varies from region to region, and even from yard to yard. In general, wet and woodland areas have acid soil, while deserts and other dry areas have alkaline soil. However, only a soil test can tell you exactly what soil pH you have (see the next section). Depending on the results, you may need to adjust the pH up or down.

Sulfur is the material most often added to the soil to lower its pH, while calcium carbonate, also called agricultural limestone (or simply lime), is added to raise it. The soil-test laboratory should advise you in writing on how much of which substance (if any) will be needed.

Once your lawn is established, you do not need to retest the soil unless a lawn expert suggests there is a pH-related problem. To evaluate the soil beneath your lawn, dig up a small patch of turf and take samples from the soil around the roots.

Soil tests   The first step in preparing any soil for a lawn is to have your soil tested. A soil test eliminates guesswork on what condition your soil is in and what amendments must be added. A soil test can provide exact information about the pH and texture of your soil, any nutrient deficiencies, and the presence of organic matter and harmful salts. Some tests can also detect the residues of herbicides or other chemicals.

Many local colleges and county offices test soils for residents of their state. If you live in a state without soil-testing programs, check the yellow pages under "Laboratories, testing" for the names of private laboratories, or ask your county extension agent for help. Some laboratories will only tell you what is wrong, while others supply instructions on how to interpret test results and take appropriate steps to improve the soil. It is best to use a laboratory that provides you with the additional information.

Here's how to take a soil sample for testing by a lab. First, obtain any necessary forms or questionnaires from your agricultural extension service or private soil lab. Typical questions include: How large is the sample area? Has fertilizer or lime ever been added? To what degree is the land sloped? and What types of plants have been grown in that area?

To collect the soil, you need a clean, non-metal bucket or container, a soil core sampler or a garden trowel or spade, pencil and paper, and a mailable container (such as a clean milk carton or a plastic bag) that holds about a pint of soil.

To get reliable soil-test results, gather the soil from several spots in the area where you are planning to install your lawn. Low spots, trouble spots, and areas with obviously different soils

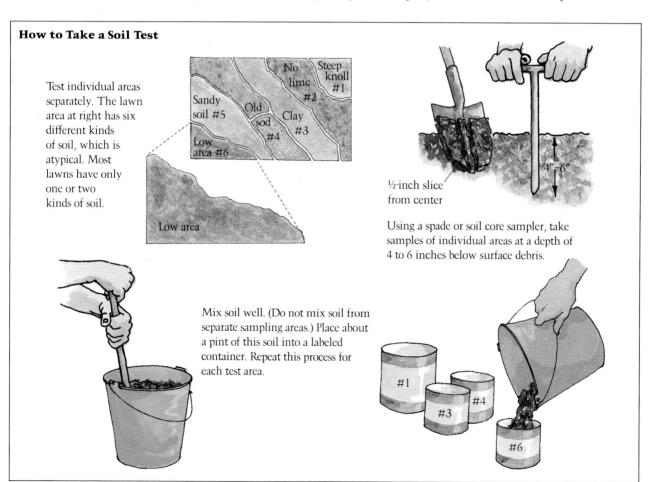

How to Take a Soil Test

Test individual areas separately. The lawn area at right has six different kinds of soil, which is atypical. Most lawns have only one or two kinds of soil.

No lime #2 / Steep knoll #1 / Sandy soil #5 / Old sod #4 / Clay #3 / Low area #6

Low area

½-inch slice from center

Using a spade or soil core sampler, take samples of individual areas at a depth of 4 to 6 inches below surface debris.

4"–6"

Mix soil well. (Do not mix soil from separate sampling areas.) Place about a pint of this soil into a labeled container. Repeat this process for each test area.

#1   #3   #4   #6

should be treated as separate sampling sites. You should take samples from discrete areas of your lawn, such as the front and back yards.

Remove soil samples with a soil core sampler, which can be purchased at a nursery or hardware store. When pushed into damp ground, this tubelike device pulls out a plug of soil about ¾ inch wide and a foot long. Remove from this plug the top 4 to 6 inches of soil below any surface debris, and place it into a bucket. If you do not have a tube, take the soil sample with a trowel or shovel, from a depth of 4 to 6 inches below surface debris.

Collect soil from four or five locations in each sampling area. Mix the soil samples in the bucket and allow them to dry. It is important that the tools you use are clean and do not have any chemical residues that might affect the samples.

Place about a pint of this soil mixture into your container, label it properly, and mail it to the soil lab. On the label, record where each set of samples was taken and include your name, address, and telephone number. Also provide the lab with any pertinent information about the history of the land. This would include known use of herbicides or soil sterilants, or any overdoses of fertilizer.

Step 2: Removing Debris

To start with, clear all debris such as wood, stones, large roots, and other items from the planting area.

Rotting wood can cause low spots in a lawn as it decomposes and can serve as a food source for termites. A tree stump, though often difficult to remove, can cause mushroom growth on the lawn above its roots. If you want to remove the stump, do it now. A tree care company can remove it for you with a stump grinder.

Stones and cement can damage rotary tillers and other equipment. It is best to pick up all you find, pile them into a wheelbarrow, and haul them away. Do not bury any debris under the future lawn.

Step 3: Controlling Weeds

Save yourself time and trouble later on by eliminating weeds now. There are three effective methods.

Use the first method in late summer, when most of the weeds have set seed. Remove existing weeds with a hoe, or spray them with a contact herbicide such as glyphosate. Water the soil every few days to germinate any weed seeds in the soil. Every week or two, as more weeds germinate, kill them by digging them up or by spraying them with glyphosate. Continue this process until no more weeds germinate, then plant the lawn.

The second method is most effective in spring and summer, when most of the weeds are actively growing. Spray the existing weeds with glyphosate. Some weed grasses such as bermudagrass and St. Augustine grass may require a second treatment after three or four weeks. Glyphosate breaks down on contact with the soil, so seeding or sodding may be done a week or two after treatment.

The third method is fumigation; it kills everything in the soil and can be done at any time. Soil fumigants can be applied by professionals to control not only weed seeds but also fungi, nematodes, and soil insects. After three weeks, test to see if the soil is safe by planting some fast-germinating seeds, such as radishes. If they sprout and begin normal growth, it is safe to sow seed or lay sod.

Weeds will invariably crop up after the new lawn is planted. When they do, pull them out by hand or allow them to grow until it is appropriate to use an herbicide. A new lawn should not be sprayed with herbicides until after the third or fourth mowing.

For more information on weed control, see pages 80 to 89.

Step 4: Establishing a Rough Grade

The purpose of rough grading is to bring the soil surface to the height and slope you want. It also promotes proper drainage.

You establish a rough grade by filling low spots and leveling hills. Most lots have fixed grade points, such as house foundations, sidewalks, driveways, and trees. When grading, both rough and finished soil (soil that has been more finely broken down) must be distributed so that the ground slopes gradually between the grade points.

Prevent water from draining toward a house foundation by establishing the grade at a 1 to 2 percent slope away from the house. That translates to about a 1- to 2-foot drop per 100 feet. A long string and a level are useful in determining the amount of slope.

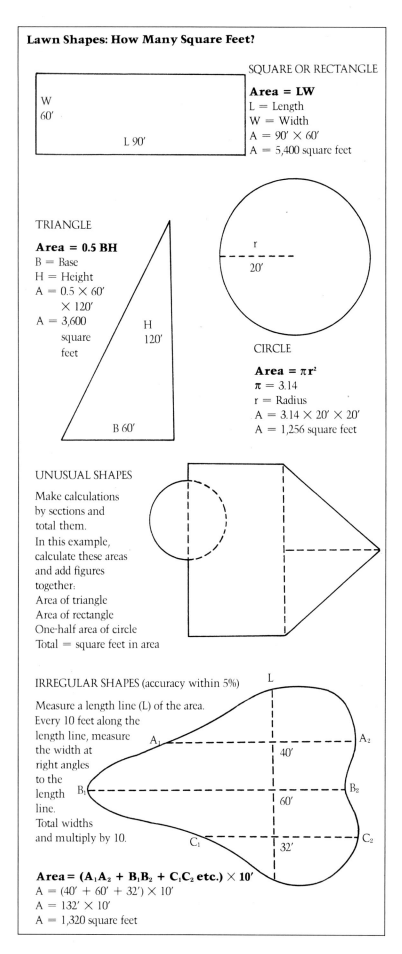

Lawn Shapes: How Many Square Feet?

SQUARE OR RECTANGLE

W
60'

L 90'

Area = LW
L = Length
W = Width
A = 90' × 60'
A = 5,400 square feet

TRIANGLE

Area = 0.5 BH
B = Base
H = Height
A = 0.5 × 60'
  × 120'
A = 3,600
  square
  feet

H
120'

B 60'

r
20'

CIRCLE

Area = πr²
π = 3.14
r = Radius
A = 3.14 × 20' × 20'
A = 1,256 square feet

UNUSUAL SHAPES

Make calculations
by sections and
total them.
In this example,
calculate these areas
and add figures
together:
Area of triangle
Area of rectangle
One-half area of circle
Total = square feet in area

IRREGULAR SHAPES (accuracy within 5%)

Measure a length line (L) of the area.
Every 10 feet along the
length line, measure
the width at
right angles
to the
length
line.
Total widths
and multiply by 10.

L

A_1 - - - - - - - - A_2
40'
B_1 - - - - - - - - B_2
60'
C_1 - - - - - C_2
32'

Area = (A_1A_2 + B_1B_2 + C_1C_2 etc.) × 10'
A = (40' + 60' + 32') × 10'
A = 132' × 10'
A = 1,320 square feet

If rough grading will be extensive, remove and stockpile the topsoil or soil amendments beforehand. This prevents them from being buried under the subsoil.

Where underlying hardpan or heavy clay soil creates poor drainage, you may need to install drain tiles. Consult a drainage contractor for advice. Drainage work should be done after the rough grading, but before adding topsoil and amendments.

Trees are sensitive to the amount of soil above their roots. Try to avoid adding or removing more than 2 inches under large trees. If you must add or remove more than this, you may need to build a tree well or retaining wall to maintain the original soil level at the foot of the tree. An experienced landscape contractor can build this for you, or you can refer to books on landscaping for instructions.

Step 5: Measuring the Lawn Area

Determine the dimensions of the lawn with a tape measure and write them down for future reference. They are helpful for estimating the amount of grass seed, sod, sprigs or plugs, and amendments you need to use. Formulas for calculating the areas of various lawn shapes appear in the illustration at the left.

Step 6: Rotary Tilling, Adding Soil Amendments

Once the grade is sloped the way you want it, add soil amendments of the type and quantity indicated in your soil-test report; or refer to the Soil Amendments chart on page 30. Soil amendments can help change the texture, pH, and nutrient content of your soil to create optimum conditions for grass growth. If your soil is hard to work, you will probably need to break it up with a rotary tiller before adding amendments.

It is important to work any amendments into the soil as thoroughly and evenly as possible, so that grass will benefit from it consistently. You can mix in the amendments with a shovel or preferably a rotary tiller (available for rent at equipment rental companies). Blend them to a depth of 6 to 8 inches, the zone where most grass roots grow. Unless you are using fresh manure or some other amendment that needs time to decompose, you can begin planting as soon as you have mixed the amendments with the soil.

You should note that the addition of large quantities of soil amendments will raise the level of the existing soil. Thus, either some of the soil should be removed first, or small sloping mounds should be made in the lawn. These mounds can often be attractive and add interest to an otherwise flat lawn.

Organic matter The best way to improve either a heavy clay soil or a light sandy soil is to add organic matter—not just a little, but a lot.

The addition of organic matter, such as compost, peat moss, composted manure, redwood sawdust, finely ground pine or fir bark, and composted rice hulls or other local agricultural by-products, makes clay soil more friable and easier to work. In clay soil, organic matter improves drainage and allows air to move into soil more readily. In sandy soil, it holds moisture and nutrients in the root zone. The more organic matter you add to a sandy soil, the more you increase its moisture-holding capacity.

Adding decomposed organic matter supplies your soil with needed nitrogen. However, fresh organic matter often causes what is known as a nitrogen draft. As the fresh organic matter decomposes in the soil, both the organisms breaking it down and the lawn roots themselves compete for nitrogen, actually causing a deficiency. Symptoms of nitrogen draft include yellowing and slowed growth of the lawn. Common inducers of nitrogen draft include fresh-ground bark, straw, and manure containing large amounts of sawdust or straw. If you are using fresh organic matter, you can compensate for nitrogen draft by thoroughly mixing 1 pound of actual nitrogen into each cubic yard of soil amendment. Ammonium sulfate fertilizer is a good source of nitrogen for this purpose. To compute the amount of actual nitrogen to use, refer to the worksheet on page 71. Or better yet, switch to a decomposed organic matter.

However, even decomposed organic matter can have its drawbacks. For example, barnyard manure and compost often contain troublesome weed seeds. Peat moss is generally expensive and does not contribute much nutrition to the soil. Aim for a final soil mixture that is about 25 percent organic matter by volume. About 2 inches of organic matter mixed into the top 6 inches of soil is usually sufficient. It is important to mix the amendments thoroughly into the existing soil. Failure to do this may

cause an interface (barrier between dissimilar soils) to form, slowing or stopping the downward movement of water. For amounts of organic matter needed to cover a lawn, see the Soil Amendments chart on page 30.

Gypsum In clay soils that are high in sodium, such as those of the arid Southwest, water has a hard time penetrating the surface and the soil may be hard to work. In these soils, gypsum (calcium sulfate) is often added to make the soil more friable.

Resembling flour in color and texture, gypsum is sold in 50-pound bags or sometimes in bulk. Depending on the percentage of clay in the soil, 100 to 350 pounds of gypsum per 1,000 square feet should be spread evenly on top of the soil and worked in with a rotary tiller or dug in with a shovel, to a depth of 6 to 8 inches. The average amount used is 200 pounds per 1,000 square feet. A soil test will normally tell you a more exact amount to use, if any.

A rotary tiller, available from equipment rental companies, speeds the work of breaking up hard soil and mixing in amendments.

Lime and sulfur If a soil test indicates that the pH of your soil is below 5.5 or above 7.5 (that is, outside the acceptable range for most grasses), you will need to adjust it. You do this by adding lime to raise the pH of acid soils, or sulfur to lower the pH of alkaline soils. Most soil-test reports will tell you exactly how much of which substance to add.

If you are preparing low-pH soil for a new lawn, the easiest and best form of lime to use is ground limestone, which works well and is widely available. Dolomitic limestone (dolomite) is the best type in many areas because it adds magnesium as well as calcium. Alternatives are pelleted limestone, hydrated lime, and ground seashells. Lime is best applied with a mechanical spreader. For information on spreaders, see pages 72 and 73.

Applying lime to the soil periodically is a way of life in areas of high rainfall, where rain has leached much of the calcium from the soil. In these areas, you probably already know that your soil needs lime. If you are not sure whether you need to add lime, check with your local nursery or have a lab test a soil sample taken from various parts of the lawn. If lime is needed, spread it evenly over the ground (or over an existing lawn), then water it.

If your soil is too alkaline, you can use a compound known as soil sulfur (also called elemental sulfur or flowers of sulfur) to make it more acid; apply it to the soil as you would

Soil Amendments

Organic Matter: Cubic Yards to Add*

Area in Square Feet	Cubic Yards to Add to 6 Inches of Soil to Achieve Desired Percentage of Organic Matter				
	10%	15%	20%	25%	30%
300	0.6	0.8	1.1	1.4	1.7
500	0.9	1.4	1.9	2.3	2.8
1,000	1.9	2.8	3.7	4.6	5.6
3,000	5.6	8.3	11.1	13.9	16.7
5,000	9.3	13.9	18.5	23.1	27.8
10,000	18.5	27.8	37.0	46.3	55.6
20,000	37.0	55.6	74.1	92.6	111.1
40,000	74.1	111.1	148.1	185.2	222.2

* One cubic yard covers 162 square feet to a depth of 2 inches.

Ground Limestone: Amounts to Raise Soil pH to 6.5

Original pH	Pounds to Add (per 1,000 square feet)**				
	Sand	Sandy Loam	Loam	Silt Loam	Clay Loam
4.0	60	115	161	193	230
4.5	51	96	133	161	193
5.0	41	78	106	129	152
5.5	28	60	78	92	106
6.0	14	32	41	51	55

** In the southern and coastal states, reduce the application by approximately one half.

Soil Sulfur: Amounts to Lower Soil pH to 6.5

Original pH	Pounds to Add (per 1,000 square feet)				
	Sand	Sandy Loam	Loam	Silt Loam	Clay Loam
8.5	46	51	57	63	69
8.0	28	31	34	40	46
7.5	11	14	18	20	23
7.0	2	3	4	5	7

lime. Other acidifying materials are ferrous sulfate, lime-sulfur solution, and fertilizers such as ammonium sulfate.

For approximate amounts of ground limestone or soil sulfur to use for correcting soil pH, see the Soil Amendments chart on page 30.

Step 7: Adding High-Phosphorus Fertilizer

Adding phosphorus to the soil encourages new lawn grass to thicken quickly by promoting strong root development. A high-phosphorus fertilizer that is also high in nitrogen, such as ammonium phosphate (which contains 16 percent nitrogen, 20 percent phosphorus, and 0 percent potassium), will help the grass green up quickly. Mix it thoroughly with the top 6 to 8 inches of soil. Make several passes with a rotary tiller in crosswise directions, to ensure that the soil, organic matter, gypsum, lime or sulfur, and fertilizer are properly blended.

A complete fertilizer containing nitrogen should be applied after the lawn becomes established, and should be repeated on a regular schedule. See page 71 for more information.

Step 8: Installing an Underground Sprinkler System (Optional)

If you live where rainfall is infrequent or unreliable, your lawn will depend on you alone for regular watering. An automatic sprinkler system, buried beneath your lawn, can free you from the chore of watering on schedule with a hose and sprinkler.

If you will be digging the trenches by hand, the time to install an underground system is just after the amendments have been worked into the soil. At this stage the soil has been loosened enough to make trench digging easier, and you will avoid potential pipe damage from tilling equipment. If you will be using power trenching equipment, however, it is easier to operate the equipment on undisturbed soil, before any amendments have been added. See pages 57 to 59 for further advice on installing a sprinkler system.

Step 9: Installing an Edging (Optional)

Edgings give a lawn a finished look. They also help keep shrubs and flowers in nearby beds from entering the lawn area, and the grass from overgrowing the plant beds. Warm-season grasses in particular have a tendency to invade nearby territory because of their creeping pattern of growth.

The most common materials used for lawn edgings are wood, poured concrete, bricks, and heavy-gauge plastic. Each has its place in the landscape; however, they vary in cost, durability, ease of installation and maintenance, and, of course, appearance.

Whatever type of edging you install, place it deep enough that the top of the edging material sits ½ inch above the finished grade. If you will be installing sod, the edging should sit 1 inch above the grade to accommodate the extra thickness of the turf. Soil on the nonlawn side of

A drop spreader distributes fertilizer evenly over the soil to help promote root development.

the edging should be graded flush with the top to help brace the edging against the impact of a lawn mower.

Step 10: Establishing the Final Grade

The purpose of creating a final (or finished) grade is to make the soil surface smooth and even enough for planting. Do this just before you plant. Use a large steel rake to comb out any remaining rocks and make the surface as even as possible. Scour large areas with a piece of chain-link fence. It is difficult to correct high and low spots later.

Step 11: Rolling and Watering

Lightly rolling the freshly prepared soil with a water-filled roller (available from a nursery or equipment rental company) firms up the area to create a more uniform planting surface for seeds. In dry areas, it also reduces dustiness by compressing the soil. Fill the roller about half full of water and push it slowly in a crossing pattern over the entire soil area. After rolling, water the area well to settle the soil.

A common problem with new lawns is that soil settles unevenly. This occurs primarily where trenches have been dug for underground sprinkler pipes. If your carefully prepared grade changes after watering, repeat steps 10 and 11 until the soil settles properly.

Now you are ready to begin planting seeds, sprigs, plugs, or sod.

SEED LAWNS

In most of North America, planting seed is the most common way to start a new lawn. One reason is that seed is so economical—it usually accounts for no more than 5 percent of the total cost of establishing a new lawn, versus 60 to 75 percent for sod. Another reason is the variety available. Although there are now more kinds of sod grass for sale than there used to be, there are still far more varieties of seed.

Buying Seed

Buy seed from a reliable source. Carefully prepared seed is healthy and has a high percentage of germination. It is also weed and disease free. Spending a few more dollars now for the best possible seed can save you hundreds of dollars in the years ahead. You can count on having fewer maintenance problems and a generally healthier lawn.

Seed for lawn grasses can be purchased in packages of a single type or in various combinations of species or varieties. The seed you select is important. Make sure that both the grass type and the particular cultivar are adapted to your climate and to the amount of sunlight in your yard. Also make certain that the grass in question can stand up to the amount of foot traffic it will receive, and can thrive under the level of care you expect to provide for it. See the Lawn Grass Comparisons chart on page 21 for a comparison of specific grasses.

Reading Seed Labels

The variety of lawn seed available in most nurseries and hardware stores can make selecting lawn seed a bewildering experience. The range of sizes, prices, and brand names is confusing enough in itself, but the many assortments of grass types, cultivars, and germination rates can make comparison especially baffling.

Understanding a seed label enables you to make an informed, wise decision. The sample seed label on page 34 shows and briefly explains the components of a typical label. The following are more detailed descriptions.

Directions for use   Most commercial mixes give you two sets of directions: one for seeding a new lawn and the other for reseeding an old lawn. There is usually a statement such as "enough seed for 1,000 square feet of new lawn or 2,000 square feet for reseeding." This helps you anticipate how far the seed will go. Some packages also indicate the spreader setting to use. If you are using a mechanical spreader, this setting makes it dispense the seed at a rate that will cover the promised area. You can buy a handheld rotary spreader inexpensively, or you can rent a drop or broadcast spreader from a nursery or equipment rental company.

The directions often include brief steps in preparing the site for seeding. (For detailed steps to site preparation, see pages 24 to 32.)

The amount of seed needed to plant a new lawn varies according to the seed size and the growth habit of the grass. Most lawns get a good start if seeded at a rate of 3 million seeds per 1,000 square feet, which equals approximately 1½ pounds of Kentucky bluegrass or 5 pounds of fine fescue over the same area.

Although cultivars of the same grass type vary in seed size, these differences are inconsequential when determining how much seed to use. For more on determining how much seed of particular varieties to use, look at the Seed Facts chart on page 35.

Fine- and coarse-textured grasses   Grasses are divided into two groups: fine textured and coarse textured. Bentgrass, bermudagrass, bluegrass, fine fescue, and perennial ryegrass are fine textured. Other grass varieties, including annual ryegrass and turf-type tall fescue, are classified as coarse textured.

Fine-textured grasses usually provide the softest-looking and most aesthetically pleasing lawns, but they are also fairly delicate when it comes to withstanding traffic. If this type of lawn is your goal, look for a mixture of lawn seed that contains at least 50 percent fine-textured grasses. If you desire a coarse-textured lawn, look for a mixture containing 40 to 50 percent coarse-textured grass.

Percentages   When a label on a box of lawn seed mix says that 60 percent of it is Kentucky bluegrass and 40 percent is red fescue, it means 60 percent and 40 percent by *weight* of the contents. To better understand what this means, take a look at the Seed Facts chart on page 35. Note that there are usually more than 2 million seeds of Kentucky bluegrass in a pound, and more than 600,000 seeds per pound of fine fescue (of which red fescue is one type). When you plant a mixture of 60 percent Kentucky bluegrass and 40 percent red fescue, in actual seed numbers you are planting 84 percent bluegrass and 16 percent red fescue. That is because a fine-fescue seed is more than three times as heavy as a Kentucky bluegrass seed. The actual content of a seed mixture would be clearer if the percentages represented seed counts rather than weight.

Germination percentages let you know what proportion of seeds of each type germinate under ideal conditions as of the test date. By multiplying the germination percentage by the percent of the grass type, you can determine what percentage of that type has the potential to grow. This calculation is called percent-pure live seed. This percentage is not listed on the label, but it is one way to figure the real value of the seed before purchasing it.

Continuing to use the mixture of 60 percent Kentucky bluegrass and 40 percent fine fescue as an example, if the germination percentage of the bluegrass is 80 percent, then 60 percent multiplied by 80 percent (.60 × .80) equals the percent-pure live seed of Kentucky bluegrass. If 90 percent of the seeds of fine fescue germinate, multiplying 90 percent by 40 percent (.90 × .40) would give you a percent-pure live seed of fescue. By these calculations, you see that the mixture is actually 48 percent Kentucky bluegrass and 36 percent red fescue by weight. As the germination percentage goes down, you are in effect buying less seed.

If a container of seed is unmixed and unblended, its label lists the percentage of purity. Effectively, this has the same meaning as the percentages of grass types in a seed mixture. A box of straight Kentucky bluegrass should be at least 90 percent pure. Multiplying the

Seed heads of tall fescue are ready to harvest for hybridizing. They will be used to create improved varieties of lawn grass.

percentage of purity by the germination percentage tells you the percentage of viable seeds in the box, and thus the value of the seed.

Percent-pure live seed is a good way to compare value, but it can be difficult to compute while you are shopping. A good but more approximate method is to compare germination percentages, crop- and weed-seed percentages, and the occurrence, if any, of noxious weeds (see the next section). Obviously, the more viable grass seeds and the fewer weed seeds there are, the better the quality.

Crop and weed seed Agricultural laws in each state distinguish between crops and weeds. Labeling laws were designed for growers, not buyers, of lawn seed. That is why some of the most serious lawn weeds may not be listed under "Weed seed." Bromegrass, orchardgrass, tall fescue, and timothy—all commercial grass crops—are serious weeds in certain contexts because they tend to invade or overseed neighboring grasses. For example, just 1 percent of a 1-pound box of tall fescue can contribute 10,000 seeds to every 1,000 square feet of new lawn.

A Sample Seed Label

This label is an example of what you find on grass seed boxes or containers. The proportions of grasses listed are only a sample. A good seed mixture is indicated by a low percentage of weed and crop seeds, an absence of noxious weeds, and high percentages of germination.

Attractive lawns depend on fine-textured grasses. Look for common, high-quality grasses here, such as Kentucky bluegrass and fine fescues.

When seed quantities account for more than 5 percent of the mixture, the label must show the state or country where the seed crop was grown. This has no bearing on grass adaptation.

Germination is the characteristic most subject to change for the worse as the seed ages. Percentages represent the amount of seed that germinates under ideal conditions. This varies with the grass.

Named cultivars are considered superior to common types and, in most cases, are a sign of a good mixture.

Percentages indicate the proportion of the grass by weight, not seed count. See Seed Facts on page 35.

Fine-Textured Grasses	Origin	Germination
30% Kentucky bluegrass	Oregon	80%
20% 'Adelphi' Kentucky bluegrass	Oregon	80%
20% 'Fylking' Kentucky bluegrass	Oregon	80%
29% Creeping red fescue	Canada	90%

Coarse Kinds	Other Ingredients
None claimed	0.01% Crop seed
	1.05% Inert matter
	0.03% Weed seed
	No noxious weeds

Tested: (No earlier than 9 months of date listed.)

These are seeds from any commercially grown grass crop. They may be other lawn grasses or problem grasses such as timothy or orchardgrass. Look for "0.00%."

Generally, "coarse kinds" tend to clump and do not mix well with other grasses. Course-textured grasses should not exceed half of the mixture. The exception is turf-type perennial ryegrass. Some kinds are listed as coarse by law, but are actually fine textured.

The chaff, dirt, and miscellaneous material that manages to escape cleaning is called inert matter. Although harmless, it should not total more than 3 or 4 percent.

It is virtually impossible to keep all weed seeds out of a seed crop, but look for less than 1 percent. State laws regulate which species of plants are considered weeds.

This is the guarantee that all the information listed on the label is correct. It is best to buy seed that shows a current date. Seed stored in a cool, dry place lasts months longer.

Noxious weeds are troublesome. In most states, it is illegal to sell seed that contains certain weeds. When present, they must be individually named and the number of seeds per ounce indicated. A good seed mixture should have none.

Seed Facts

	Seeds per Pound	Pounds of Seed per 1,000 sq. ft.	Minimum % Purity	Minimum % Germination	Days to Germinate*
Bahiagrass	175,000	8–10	75	70	21–28
Creeping bentgrass	6,500,000	½–1	98	90	4–12
Common bermudagrass	1,750,000	1–2	97	85	10–30
Blue grama	800,000	1–3	40	70	15–30
Kentucky bluegrass	2,200,000	1–2	90	80	14–30
Buffalograss	290,000	2	85	75	14–30
Centipedegrass	410,000	1–2	50	70	14–20
Fine fescues	615,000	2–5**	97	90	7–14
Tall fescue	230,000	6–10	97	90	7–12
Annual ryegrass	230,000	5–10	97	90	5–10
Perennial ryegrass	230,000	5–10	97	90	5–10

* Varies according to growing conditions.
** Chewings fescue: 5 lbs. Hard fescue: 3½–4½ lbs. Red fescue: 2–4 lbs.

Thus you can see that a small percentage of these can establish many weeds.

The percentage of weed seeds in a package of lawn seed can represent a few harmless weeds with large seeds or many serious weeds with small seeds. The quality of the producer is the only standard by which to judge this. For example, in a 1-pound seed package with 0.27 percent weeds, a homeowner might unknowingly be planting 5,400 seeds of annual bluegrass—a nuisance grass of which there are about 2 million seeds per pound.

Noxious weeds Noxious weeds are those that tend to be especially difficult to eliminate once they are established. Many spread just as aggressively by runners or bulbs as they do by seed. Each state has a list of weeds it considers noxious, and there is a national list as well.

The noxious weeds specified in the Federal Seed Act are white-top (*Lepedium draba, L. repens, Hymenosphysa pubescens*); Canada thistle (*Cirsium arvense*); dodder (*Cuscuta* species); quackgrass (*Agropyron repens*); johnsongrass (*Sorghum halepense*); bindweed (*Convovulus arvensis*); Russian knapweed (*Centaurea repens*); perennial sowthistle (*Sonchus arvensis*); and leafy spurge (*Euphorbia esula*). Most are field crop weeds, but a few are serious lawn weeds.

Bermudagrass (*Cynodon dactylon*) and annual bluegrass (*Poa annua*) are considered noxious weeds in a few states. If present in a seed mixture, noxious weeds must be named

and the number of seeds per ounce shown. In a high-quality seed mixture, there should be none.

Straights, Mixtures, and Blends

Grass seed is sold in three types of assortments: straights, mixtures, and blends. The type to choose depends on the kind of lawn you want.

Straights This refers to containers of lawn seed that are composed of just one type of grass. Many warm-season lawns consist of only one variety, because most warm-season grasses invade neighboring grasses so readily that there is no point in combining them. Lawns of common bermudagrass and St. Augustine grass are examples of this. Tall fescue and bentgrass are cool-season grasses that are sometimes used alone. Tall fescue is invasive by nature (and sometimes considered a weed), and bentgrass has a unique fine texture that looks best when grown by itself. A lawn of a single variety can look uniform and attractive, but it is more vulnerable to disease, so think twice before planting a lawn with a single variety.

Mixtures A mixture contains seed from two or more types of grass species, such as coarse textured, turf type, or cool season. The strength of one grass type compensates for the weakness of another. For this reason, a mixture is best for the average lawn. For most climates, the best mixtures are insect and disease resistant and have broader overall adaptability.

The grasses that mix together best have similar colors, textures, and growth rates, and are roughly equal in aggressiveness. Grasses that are similar in these respects are Kentucky bluegrass, fine fescues, and perennial ryegrass. Seed formulators vary the proportions of these ingredients and sometimes add small amounts of other grasses, depending on the intended use of the mixture. For instance, they add more fine fescue for lawns with partial shade and for drought-prone soil. They mix in more perennial ryegrass to get the lawn off to a fast start. And they add quantities of Kentucky bluegrass to produce a show lawn.

Blends   A blend is a combination of cultivars from one species of grass. The benefit of blending cultivars is that it usually produces a lawn with improved resistance to certain diseases while preserving the texture and color of the particular type of grass. For example, a combination of 'Adelphi', 'Baron', and 'Rugby' Kentucky bluegrasses is a blend. Occasionally, a seed container states that it is "an all-bluegrass mixture." Since this "mixture" has only one type of grass, it is technically a blend. If you are looking for a mixture instead of a blend, remember that a true mixture has more than one species of grass.

Seed Ratings

Almost every state has a program of seed certification. Technically, certified seed only guarantees the purity of each cultivar. In other words, if the label says "Certified 'Adelphi' Kentucky bluegrass," the package is guaranteed to contain 'Adelphi' Kentucky bluegrass. In most states, certification also guarantees that there are fewer weed seeds, other crop contaminants, and inert fillers than would be found in uncertified seed.

"Percent fluorescence" is a special rating for perennial ryegrass. In 1929, researchers discovered that annual ryegrass (a less desirable grass with similar seeds) secretes a fluorescent substance when it germinates on white filter paper. Modern perennial ryegrasses do not secrete this substance.

To certify the purity of perennial ryegrass, manufacturers germinate a sample on filter paper. If any fluorescence appears when the sample is exposed to ultraviolet light, the presence of annual ryegrass (or a hybrid of annual

and perennial ryegrass) is established. By law, there can be no more than 3 percent fluorescence in a bag of seeds. Not all manufacturers require this test of quality to be indicated on the seed label. If listed, the percentage of any fluorescing seedlings is included under "Other Ingredients" on a seed label.

From Germination to Establishment

Once seeds are in the ground, their ability to germinate and eventually form a full lawn depends on several factors: the availability of moisture, the type of grass, its germination rate, its initial growth rate, and the day-to-day temperature. Germination can take anywhere from 4 to 30 days, with an average of 14 to 21 days, followed by a 6- to 10-week establishment period prior to use. When you sow seed, keep in mind that seed invariably germinates more slowly in the cool temperatures of early spring (or in mild climates, late fall). This slowness notwithstanding, cool periods are the most appropriate times to plant; you will simply need to wait a little longer for the lawn to fill in.

HOW TO SEED A LAWN

Before you start to seed your lawn, lay out its boundaries and prepare the soil as described on pages 24 to 32. Since newly seeded areas need to be kept constantly moist, be sure you have a way to water the new lawn area thoroughly and evenly. Next, calculate the amount of seed you will need for the lawn you plan to install (see the Seed Facts chart on page 35). Assemble the necessary tools and supplies beforehand to prevent unwanted delays.

Now sow the seed. You can cover large lawns with the same equipment used to spread fertilizer. In small areas you can easily sow the seed by hand. Regardless of the seeding method, divide the seed into two equal lots. Sow the first lot across the lawn in rows; then sow the second lot in rows at right angles to the first until the whole lawn is crisscrossed with seeds. If you are using a wheeled spreader, calibrate it to deliver seeds at half the recommended rate in each direction, so that you do not overseed. You may need to touch up edges by hand.

After seeding, ensure good contact between seed and soil by lightly raking the entire area. Do not rake too roughly; if you do, you will redistribute seed, ruin the final grade, and bury the seed too deeply. Seeding at a depth of ⅛ to ¼ inch (depending on seed size) is usually sufficient. To establish this depth and to place seeds firmly into the soil, go over the area with a water-filled roller. Surrounding the seeds with soil causes the seeds to assimilate more water, which quickens germination time.

Mulching the area where grass seed has been sown hastens germination by keeping the soil moist. It also helps keep birds from eating the seeds. On slopes, partially covering the seeded area with a mulch can prevent soil erosion during watering and rainfall. Many materials, such as compost, manure, topsoil, or commercially packaged mulch (often referred to as top dressing), can be used as a mulch. Wind is often a problem with lightweight mulches such as sawdust and peat moss; keeping the mulch moist will help prevent it from blowing away. In areas of strong winds or abundant rainfall, a mulch of heavier compost

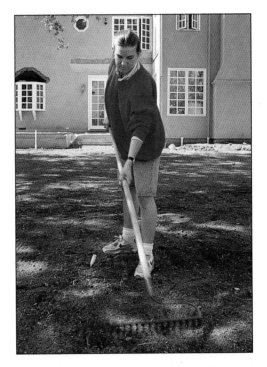

Top left: Grass seed is distributed over the lawn area with a drop spreader.
Top right: The seed is raked in to ensure good contact with the soil.
Bottom left: After raking, a water-filled roller is pushed over the planted area to firm it.
Bottom right: The seedbed is covered with a protective layer of mulch.

or topsoil is preferable. Whichever mulch you use, the covering should be approximately ¼ inch thick and applied as evenly as possible.

For seeds to germinate evenly, the top layer of soil—always the first to dry out—must stay constantly moist. Thoroughly soak to a 6-inch depth after sowing, then lightly sprinkle by hand or with an automatic sprinkler system, as often as three to four times daily until the young grass is established. Water more frequently if it is hot or windy. Use a fine spray or a nozzle with a mist setting to minimize the movement of soil and the washing away of seeds. Avoid standing water. Stringing the area with brightly colored flags will warn neighbors and children, but not necessarily dogs, to stay off.

Top: Keeping the soil moist ensures even germination.
Bottom: If conditions are right, the lawn will be lush and green in about two months.

SPRIG AND PLUG LAWNS

In areas of the country where warm-season grasses predominate, sprigging and plugging are common methods of starting a lawn. This is because the warm-season grasses grown in these regions are creeping grasses that spread vigorously. Both sprigging and plugging are economical methods of using sod.

Sprigs (also called stolons or runners) are pieces of torn-up sod of creeping grasses; planting them is similar to seeding in that large quantities are spread over an area. The sprigs are set several inches apart and eventually grow together. Plugs are small squares or circles of sod that are also planted at intervals. Grasses planted by either method spread by rhizomes or stolons that run parallel to the soil surface to root and sprout as new plants. For warm-season grasses that do not set viable seed, such as hybrid bermudagrass, these are the only planting methods.

Unlike seeds, which need time to grow from the ground up, the sprigs or plugs take hold immediately and begin generating more plants from rhizomes and stolons. In a fairly short time they fill in to form an even lawn.

Sprigging and plugging are not practiced with most cool-season grasses, such as Kentucky bluegrass, fescues, or ryegrasses, because

Sprigs of warm-season grass are set into the soil to spread vigorously by rhizomes and stolons.

The sprigs creep over bare ground, eventually filling it in.

they lack the creeping growth habit that would enable them to spread quickly.

Before planting sprigs or plugs, prepare the soil as described on pages 24 to 32.

Sprigs

Sprigs can be short or long stemmed, with either an intact root system or two to four nodes (joints) from which roots can develop. Sprigging is simply the planting of individual sprigs at spaced intervals. Hybrid bermudagrass and centipedegrass are the ones most commonly planted by this method.

You can buy sprigs by the bushel, or you can buy sod and carefully pull or tear it apart into separate sprigs. Sprigs bought by the bushel by mail order are shipped in bags or cartons. Shipping usually takes place within 24 hours after the sod has been mechanically shredded. Sprigs can sometimes also be purchased from nurseries in areas where warm-season grasses are commonly planted.

The best time to plant sprigs is from late spring to midsummer. The onset of warmer weather provides optimum growing conditions for warm-season grasses.

The soil should be ready to plant when the sprigs arrive. Keep the sprigs cool and moist until planting time, which should be as soon as possible after delivery. It takes only five minutes of sunlight to damage sprigs enclosed in plastic bags. Even when stored properly, sprigs decay rapidly.

How to plant sprigs   There are several ways to plant sprigs. Whichever method you use, it is always best to work with *slightly* moist soil. In any case, *do not let the stems dry out.* Water sections as you plant them, and keep the soil constantly moist until the stems are established.

One planting method is to cut 2- to 3-inch-deep furrows in the soil bed and place the sprigs in the furrows. Dig the furrows with a hoe and space them from 4 to 12 inches apart, depending on the rate of coverage you would like. Close spacing results in more rapid coverage, but naturally involves more material and labor. Place the stems against one side of the furrow so that any tufts of foliage are aboveground and the light-colored stem is below ground. Firm the soil around each stem and level the area as well as possible. Rolling over the planting area with a half-filled roller helps bring the sprigs into contact with the soil and aids in the leveling.

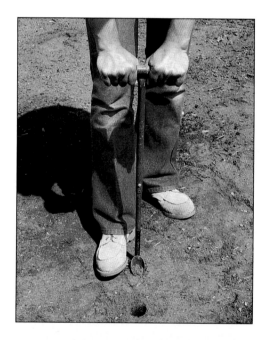

Top: A steel plugger is used to remove cores of soil for plugs. Bottom: Sod plugs are set into the holes and eventually grow together.

Another method of planting sprigs is to place the stems on the soil at desired intervals and lightly press them in with a notched stick.

The third and fastest method is called broadcast sprigging, stolonizing, or shredding. Sprigs are shredded into short stems and spread by hand over the designated area like a mulch. They are then covered with soil and rolled lightly with a water roller. No matter which planting method you choose, keep the area moist until the sprigs start growing.

Depending on the soil, sunlight, water, spacing, grass type, and other variables, a sprigged lawn takes two months to two years to fill in completely.

Plugs

Plugging is exactly what it sounds like—plugging small squares or circles of sod into the soil at regular intervals. Square plugs are cut from sod with a shovel or knife; round plugs are cut with a special steel plugger similar to a bulb planter. You may buy sod and cut the plugs yourself, but it is easier to order precut plugs by mail. The 2- to 4-inch plugs come in trays of 18, which will plant about 50 square feet. They have a root system that will quickly establish itself. Plugging is generally used only for warm-season grasses, such as centipedegrass, St. Augustine grass, and zoysiagrass.

Plant plugs just before spring weather begins. It is critical to prepare the soil correctly before the plugs arrive, for they need to be planted as quickly as possible. Although they have soil and roots of their own, they can dry out rapidly. If you anticipate a delay in planting, keep them moist by covering them with plastic away from direct sunlight.

How to plant plugs Before the plugs arrive, use a steel plugger (or a trowel or small shovel) to make holes of the proper size; usually 1 inch wider and deeper than the plugs themselves. Space the holes 6 to 12 inches apart, depending on the size of the plugs and type of grass (see pages 17 to 19). Of the warm-season grasses used for plugging, bahiagrass and bermudagrass spread the fastest, and centipedegrass and zoysiagrass spread the slowest. Gauge planting distances accordingly. To help the lawn take hold evenly, offset the rows of plugs in a checkerboard pattern. Soil taken from planting holes should be spread evenly over the ground between the holes.

When the plugs arrive, lightly moisten the soil and then place the plugs into the holes. Firm the soil around them so that the crowns of the plants (the points where leaf blades converge at the soil line) are level with the ground.

Then roll and water the plugs. Although plugs do not dry out as fast as sprigs, keeping the soil around them moist is still important. Water them daily for the first two weeks so that they do not dry out. Then, depending on the weather, you can water every other day for a month or until the plugs are well established, their roots firmly knitted with the soil below. To check for this, carefully tug on a plug. If it is hard to pull up easily, you know that the roots have taken hold.

When the plugs have established themselves, mowing should begin. Frequent mowing will stimulate the growth of stolons along the soil, making the grass spread more rapidly. The plugs can be fertilized every 6 to 8 weeks until the entire planted area has filled in. The closer together the plugs were planted, the sooner the lawn will cover the area.

After plugging, watering and rain may cause the soil to wash out between plugs, yielding an uneven and bumpy lawn. Once the roots have taken firm hold but before the plants begin to spread, you will probably need to add extra soil between the plugs to level the lawn.

Plugging is the slowest method of establishing a lawn. (Unlike sprigs, which start out stretched prone across the soil, the grass in plugs must take extra time to extend itself by sending out new rhizomes and stolons.) Zoysiagrass, the major species propagated by plugging, may take two years to fill in a lawn.

SOD LAWNS

Sod is turf that is grown commercially, cut into strips, and lifted intact, along with a thin layer of soil held together by runners, roots, or netting. Installing a sod lawn is much like laying a carpet, with the objective of reestablishing the grass roots in well-prepared soil.

Compared with establishing a lawn by seeding, sprigging, or plugging, laying sod yields quick results. A sod lawn can be functional in as little as three weeks (versus two months to two years with the other methods), although there should be some restraint on its use until its roots have knitted properly with the soil beneath. You can check on the progress of this by lifting corners of the sod.

Whereas timing is critical in seeding a lawn, a sod lawn can be installed at almost any time of the year as long as weather permits and water is available. Ideal times to install sod are in late summer, early fall, and early spring for cool-season grasses; late spring and early summer for warm-season grasses.

One advantage of sod is that it can be installed in places where a seed lawn may be difficult to establish, such as a heavily trafficked area or a slope that erodes easily. Another advantage is that it usually does not take

A pallet of sod is delivered to a site for installation. Sod should be ordered in advance so that it arrives just in time for planting.

a great deal of care to establish. Other than keeping it moist until its roots knit securely with the soil below it, you need not be concerned right away about weeds growing in the lawn, birds eating seeds, or areas of grass being washed out.

The major drawbacks of a sod lawn are the initial cost and labor, which are substantial compared with those of a seed lawn. You must weigh these costs against the benefits of achieving such fast results. Another disadvantage of sod is that it may bring with it a type of soil that is different from that in your yard. This can sometimes prevent the sod from bonding well with your soil.

Installing sod is not difficult, but it requires patient work and the strength to move heavy rolls of turf. Whether you plan to install the sod yourself or hire professionals to do it for you, you should learn as much as possible about the entire procedure beforehand.

Quality sod is uniformly thick and green, with neatly cut edges. It unrolls into 6- to 9-foot strips.

Selecting the Sod

Both cool-season and warm-season grasses are sold as sod, although many more cool-season grasses are available in this form. If the sod is made up of a mixture of grasses, it usually includes both shade-tolerant and sun-loving types to allow leeway in planting.

The first step is to select a high-quality, healthy grass that is well adapted to your area and site. Most nurseries have information on ordering the sod you want. It is important to buy sod of a variety that has been thoroughly tested in your area. Sod that has been grown at a farm near you usually has a better chance of thriving, since it is accustomed to an environment similar to yours. Given the time, energy, and expense you will be devoting to preparing your soil properly, it pays to buy only sod of highest quality.

Sod normally comes in rolled or folded strips measuring 6 to 9 feet long and 2 feet wide. Each strip weighs between 30 and 40 pounds. When you receive a delivery of sod (or pick it up at a nursery or sod farm), the strips should be moist but not too wet, and definitely not too dry. High-quality sod will be uniformly green and evenly thick from one end to the other. The grass blades should be dense and mowed to a uniform length. The edges should be cleanly cut so that they will fit together evenly. Quality sod growers maintain very high standards and deliver sod that has virtually no diseases or weeds. Do not buy any sod that has poor color or yellowing areas. These may signal that the sod is not the freshest; ideally, sod should be planted within 24 hours of harvesting.

If you have ordered the sod in advance and have had it delivered, you will not have the chance to pick it out yourself, and the shipment may be awkward to inspect when it arrives. It is therefore critical to buy from a high-quality supplier who will accept the return of inferior sod.

The thickness of sod varies, but in general the layer of soil beneath the grass blades should measure ½ to 1 inch thick. If the soil layer is too thick, the sod will root poorly or take a long time to knit with the underlying soil; if it is too thin, the sod will dry out too fast. The sod should not fall apart easily when handled. Some sod growers use a plastic netting that is incorporated in the soil to reduce the time it takes to produce a salable crop. The netting helps hold soil and grass together, but

Planting a Lawn on a Slope

Establishing a lawn on sloping ground can be difficult, especially when the grade is steep. Seed or sod can wash downhill if watered too much before it is firmly established.

When planting grass on a slope, it is important to cultivate and amend the soil to as great a depth as possible. This allows the roots to grow more deeply and encourages water to sink in rather than run off.

If you are starting your lawn from seed, sow the seeds a bit more heavily than you would for a level lawn, as some may be washed downhill by watering. If possible, rake the soil crosswise, creating tiny ridges that can help prevent seeds from washing downhill. While the seeds are germinating, water frequently but sparingly. This helps keep the topsoil from being disturbed while the seeds are taking root.

Hydroseeding is a method sometimes used for planting lawn seeds on slopes. The seed is mixed with a paper mulch and water and then sprayed through a hose onto the seedbed. This eliminates the need to spread topsoil or other material over the seed to keep it moist and in place. Lawns planted by this method need to be kept watered while they are becoming established, just as ordinary seed lawns do.

If you are laying sod on a slope, start from the lowest point and move uphill from there. Always lay the sod so that it runs perpendicular to the slope. Stagger the joints to avoid excess erosion during watering or heavy rain. On steep slopes, pegging or staking sod strips to the soil is advisable until the sod has had a chance to take hold. Use soft pine pegs, which will decompose quickly when left in place. Three pegs 6 to 8 inches long are usually sufficient to hold each strip of sod. Place one peg in each top corner and one in the center. Drive in the pegs so that they stand upright rather than at an angle.

---

it can cause problems over time. If the grass wears thin, the netting can become exposed, looking unsightly and potentially tangling up in lawn mowers or other equipment. If the sod you purchase contains netting, make sure that the soil is completely level when you plant it. This will help prevent high spots from wearing thin and exposing the netting.

Some states have a sod certification program to ensure that sod is labeled correctly and is relatively free of insects, weeds, and diseases. If certified sod is not available, make sure the sod you buy originates from a reputable sod farm. These farms usually guarantee the quality of their product and provide information on the planting and care of your new sod lawn.

Preparing the Soil

Before the sod is delivered, prepare the soil thoroughly, following the instructions on pages 24 to 32. Do not be fooled into thinking that because the sod already has soil attached, soil preparation is not important. It is just as important as it is with establishing a seed, sprig, or plug lawn.

When you are preparing the soil, note that the final grade should be 1 inch lower than you want the lawn to be. This is ½ inch lower than you would grade the soil when planting seed, plugs, or sprigs. This allows the thickness of the sod to fit flush with the tops of sprinklers, sidewalks, driveways, and edgings.

If the proper amounts of fertilizer have been worked into the soil during site preparation, it is not usually necessary to fertilize again for six weeks unless the lawn starts turning lighter green or yellowish. If fertilizer has not yet been added, evenly spread a high-phosophorus fertilizer on top of the soil so it can be readily available to the sod roots.

Ordering Sod

Order sod about one week before the planting date. This allows the grower time to schedule cutting, or the local nursery time to order the sod from its supplier.

It is not difficult to estimate the amount of sod to buy. Simply measure your lawn and calculate its square footage. (If your lawn space is not rectangular, you can use the formulas on page 28.) The nursery or sod grower will calculate how many rolls of sod you need. Buy that amount, plus 5 to 10 percent more to be sure you have enough.

Installation

Sod is usually delivered on pallets to the site where it is to be installed. When the sod arrives, have the pallets stacked in a cool, shaded area and be sure to keep the exposed soil of the outer pieces moist. If there will be more than a

Top: Starting from a straight edge, strips of sod are laid side by side across the lawn area.
Bottom: Edges should meet squarely. Use fingers to firm them together.

24-hour delay in planting, you can store sod indefinitely by unrolling it on a hard, shaded surface, such as the floor of a garage or carport, and watering it frequently.

Lay sod on moist soil. If the soil is dry, wet it a day or so before the sod is delivered to provide adequate time for it to dry to a moist stage. Avoid laying sod after a heavy rain, since the soil may be sloppy and uneven.

The easiest way to begin laying sod is to start near a straight edge, such as a sidewalk or driveway. If you have an irregularly shaped lawn, draw a straight line through it or string a line across it, and start laying sod on either side of it.

The rolls of sod are heavy—each strip can weigh 30 to 40 pounds. If possible, have two or three assistants ready to help unload the rolls as soon as they arrive. Handle the sod strips carefully to avoid tearing or stretching them. When rolling out the sod strips, stand or kneel on a board or piece of plywood to distribute your weight evenly.

Because a single roll of sod will probably not cover the length of your lawn, you will have to lay several rolls end to end. After laying each roll, place the loose end of the next roll tightly against the end of the previously laid strip and carefully unroll it. When you have filled in your lawn with one row of sod strips, start the next one. Stagger the ends of sod strips, much as a bricklayer staggers bricks. To reduce drying, keep sod edges in the closest contact possible without overlapping. Firm the edges together with your fingers, but do not stretch the sod.

The entire soil area should be covered with sod, leaving no soil bare. If you need to, cut pieces from a separate roll to fill in at ends of the lawn or in irregularly shaped areas. (But do not place small pieces or narrow strips along the edges of the lawn, because they will dry out quickly.) Make sure that all edges abut cleanly.

Along curved edges or unusually shaped areas, cut with a sharp knife or garden spade to custom-fit the turf. A knife with a serrated edge, such as an old bread knife, works well. So does a curve-bladed linoleum knife. As mentioned previously, begin laying sod in a straight line, and work toward irregular areas.

If built-in sprinkler heads have been installed, simply roll the sod over them and carefully cut a circle through the sod to expose

Extra lengths of sod can be cut away with a sharp knife.

each head. There should be no gap between the sprinkler head and the surrounding sod.

After all the sod has been laid, roll it with a water-filled roller to ensure good contact between sod roots and underlying soil. Roll perpendicular to the length of the strips.

Foot traffic can slow or damage the establishment of a sod lawn. To help prevent this, surround the area with stakes, string, and bright flags.

Watering

Once the sod has been rolled, water it thoroughly. Proper watering is the single most important step in the establishment of a sod lawn. (If the lawn area is large or the weather is warm, you should roll and water each section as it is laid; this will keep the sod from drying out.) The soil underneath should be wet to a depth of 6 to 8 inches. From then on, watch your new lawn closely. The edges of the sod strips and pieces along sidewalks and driveways are the first to dry out and the last to knit with the soil. They may require spot watering every day, perhaps even more often in hot weather. Make sure the underlying soil stays constantly moist for at least the first two weeks after planting. Once the lawn begins to knit with the soil, you can begin to approach a normal watering schedule (see page 51).

An inch of water over the area is usually sufficient to wet the soil and the sod. If you have an irrigation system, check it periodically for good coverage, especially on windy days.

After rolling, the finished lawn should be kept moist until the sod knits with the soil beneath.

You can do this by turning the system on and observing how well each sprinkler head covers its assigned area. If coverage is inadequate, clean out any defective nozzles and adjust their reach by turning them slightly. If this does not work, you may need to replace them.

After 10 to 14 days of conscientious watering, the sod should have knitted to the soil below. Signs of this are growing grass and firm resistance when you tug at a corner of the lawn (don't tug at the same corner repeatedly, or the grass there may never take root). Once the sod has taken hold, you may begin to reduce the watering time.

Lawn Care

Regular care is the key to an attractive and healthy lawn. This chapter helps you simplify the processes of watering, mowing, fertilizing, aerating, and dethatching.

Many gardeners enjoy working with their lawns. They find that getting outdoors on a Saturday is the perfect opportunity to get some sunshine while they mow and water the grass. For them, a few minutes of weed pulling during the week serves as a welcome transition from the bustle of the day's work to the calmer atmosphere of home.

But for other homeowners, lawn care is an unwelcome chore. Because they may have exaggerated notions about how much time lawn care takes, they may neglect their lawns—and then have to do even more work as a result.

The fact is that taking good care of a lawn often involves little more work than taking poor care of it. The difference between good and poor care is not in the amount of effort expended, but in *how* it is expended.

In this chapter you will learn to judge how much maintenance your lawn needs, and how to apply your effort wisely so that your lawn stays looking fit.

This fine lawn has been mowed in crossing directions to create a pleasing checkerboard pattern. A grass catcher bag on the mower saves time by picking up leaves and clippings as it goes.

Paradoxical though it may seem, regular mowing actually saves time for those following a minimal lawn-care schedule. That's because midlength grass needs less watering than longer grass.

HOW MUCH CARE DOES YOUR LAWN NEED?

Lawns are like other living things in that the more effort you devote to them, the more benefits and enjoyment you will eventually derive. If you have a lot of free time and enjoy lawn work, you can have a lawn that looks as good as any golf green. However, if there are many demands on your time, you may need to choose a more limited program that gives you a less lush-looking lawn.

The following are descriptions of three levels of lawn maintenance and what is involved at each level. Do not choose a maintenance program based on wishful thinking, but rather one that reflects a realistic appraisal of your time and inclinations.

Whatever program you choose, remember that the key is consistency. Bursts of lavish attention followed by periods of total neglect will do a lawn more harm than will a program of consistent low maintenance. It is helpful to set up a regular schedule of lawn care and to keep a record of the monthly, semiannual, and annual tasks to be accomplished. To remind you of your lawn's needs, mark on your yearly calendar the dates when you will need to apply fertilizer or perform aeration and other infrequent tasks. For reference in future years, record the dates when you applied herbicides or insect and disease controls. Like a maintenance schedule for a car, a written schedule for the lawn can help prevent more serious problems from arising.

Minimal

At the very least, a lawn needs mowing and edging on a regular basis. In areas where rainfall is sparse, most lawns should also be watered as necessary. Typically this is at least once every one to two weeks, depending on the variety of grass, the average temperature, and the moisture retentiveness of your soil. Regular mowing, supplemented by watering as needed, will help keep the lawn fairly green and actively growing, as it stimulates the grass to grow back again.

You may think that allowing your lawn to grow longer between cuttings will reduce your work by enabling you to mow less frequently. This is true, but the trouble is that taller grass requires more water than shorter grass. When rainfall is sparse, you will have to spend more time watering. So all things considered, mowing at the middle of the recommended range of cutting heights is best (see the Mowing Heights chart on page 61).

Unless the lawn is growing in fertile, well-drained soil, it needs at least an occasional application of complete lawn fertilizer, such as 15-5-10, containing iron along with the nitrogen, phosphorus, and potassium. An acceptable minimum schedule is two or three times a year—in early spring, early summer, and early fall. (If you fertilize only twice a year, omit the summer feeding.) You can achieve longer-lasting results by using a timed-release fertilizer, described on page 69. Although this type of fertilizer does not provide as quick a "green-up" effect, it does keep a lawn greener longer.

The amount of fertilizer to use, and the best methods of application, are listed on the fertilizer label; see pages 67 to 73 for more information on fertilizing. If you neglect fertilizing completely, your lawn will lose its dark green color, its overall vigor will decline, and it will be more susceptible to infestations of weeds, insects, and diseases—making lawn care much more difficult.

Moderate

A lawn maintained at a moderate level also needs regular care, but at more frequent intervals. Mow and edge as needed—that is, when the grass looks untidy or gets to be one-third higher than the recommended height for that grass (see the Mowing Heights chart on page 61). Water as needed, usually at least weekly in the absence of rainfall, depending on the variety of grass, the temperature, and the type of soil.

The lawn should also receive applications of a complete fertilizer (such as 15-5-10), at least four or five times during the period when it is actively growing. This is usually from March through October in most of the United States. If you use a timed-release fertilizer, you can get

away with fertilizing less frequently; see pages 69 and 70 for a description of these products.

Taking time to control weeds is an important part of moderate lawn care as well. The absence of weeds not only keeps the lawn more attractive, but also enables it to grow more vigorously, since a weed-free lawn does not have to compete with weeds for water, nutrients, and space. Several products are available that can fertilize the lawn and kill weeds at the same time. These can be real time-savers; see page 70. It is also possible to apply products that kill weed seeds as they germinate, thus denying them the opportunity to grow and mature. These products are known as preemergent herbicides and are discussed more fully on page 81. Lawn weeds can also be removed by hand, but this can be very time-consuming.

A moderately maintained lawn needs aerating every two years or so to penetrate thatch and open up compacted soil so that air and water can enter freely. To do this you use a specialized tool to punch numerous small holes in the lawn. See pages 75 and 76 for information.

Although these maintenance steps require additional time and energy to carry out, they help produce a lawn that needs little extra maintenance in the long run because it is in good overall health.

Lawns maintained at a moderate level should be fertilized four to five times per growing season. This gardener is applying liquid fertilizer with a hose-end sprayer.

Intensively maintained lawns should be aerated and dethatched regularly. A power-driven coring aerator can make the work easier.

Lawn Care Shortcuts

Saving time on lawn maintenance is the goal of many busy homeowners. Here are the most important things you can do to maintain your lawn efficiently.

• Care for your lawn consistently. This includes mowing and edging at the proper height, fertilizing, and keeping an eye out for weeds, insects, and diseases. It also includes regular watering in the absence of rainfall.

• Fertilize your lawn regularly, using products containing nitrogen, phosphorus, potassium, secondary nutrients, and trace elements. These benefit both the roots and the top growth of the lawn. See pages 67 to 73 for information on the types of fertilizer and how to apply them.

• Use a preemergent herbicide to keep weeds from sprouting. This can save you many hours of pulling or spraying weeds that have started to grow. Your past experience with weeds can tell you whether a preemergent herbicide

is necessary and when best to apply it. See page 81 for more about preemergent herbicides.

• Aerate your lawn as needed, normally once every year or two, or when the lawn appears to be losing its vigor. This procedure greatly benefits most grasses, helping to keep them open to air, water, and fertilizer. See pages 75 and 76 for instructions.

• Mow and edge your lawn in an efficient order. First, run the edger along the pavement and any edgings. Then mow, using a mower with a catch bag or composting setting. This takes care of clippings from the edging and mowing operations at the same time.

• Use quality lawn tools and equipment. Maintain and store them properly, and they will provide you with many years of service.

• Ask for help if you need it. Good resources are local nursery personnel, landscape contractors, lawn care professionals, horticulture instructors, and agricultural extension services.

Intensive

Consistency is important at all levels of lawn care, but it is particularly so at the intensive level. This maintenance level involves keeping a close eye on the health and appearance of your lawn to determine whether it is stressed in any way, or whether insects, weeds, or diseases are beginning to take hold. It also involves looking out for thatch buildup, which can obstruct the passage of water and nutrients into the lawn (see page 76). By watching closely for these occurrences, you will probably find yourself acting on them more frequently—and thus expending somewhat more effort than you would for a moderately maintained lawn.

Of course, a lawn that is intensively cared for should receive regular watering, mowing and trimming at the proper height, prompt treatment for weeds, and monthly applications of a complete fertilizer during seasons of active growth. Lawns also need an occasional dose of iron if the fertilizer does not include it.

The lawn should be sprayed for insects and diseases as soon as signs of these appear. Regular aerating (page 75) and dethatching (page 76), and renovation as needed (page 108), are other components of an intensive program.

All this may seem like a long list of tasks to perform in quest of a beautiful lawn, but it is important to remember that lawns are made up of thousands of grass plants. Even at this high level of maintenance, you are still devoting far less time per plant than you normally would for the other plants in your yard.

WATERING

In many parts of the United States and Canada, frequent rainfall supplies lawns with all the water they need. But in parts of the West, where months may elapse between rains, lawns need watering in order to survive. Even some normally rainy regions experience drought occasionally, making watering necessary.

Knowing how much water to apply and how often would be simple if there were set rules for every situation. But too many variables are possible. The water requirements of your lawn depend on a number of things: the type of soil you have, seasonal temperatures, wind velocity, humidity, the frequency of rain, the type of grass, and maintenance practices.

Even with all these factors to consider, however, there are certain guidelines that apply to any watering program. By combining these with your own watering experience and a knowledge of the climate in your area, you can develop a good watering program for your lawn.

How Often to Water?

The answer to this question is simply: when your lawn needs it. Water when the soil begins to dry out, before the grass wilts. When a lawn wilts, grass blades either roll or fold, exposing the bottoms of the blades. At this stage, the lawn color appears to change from a bright green to a dull blue-green or smoky color. You are actually seeing the bottoms of the wilted blades, which are grayer than the tops. This first occurs in the most drought-prone spots, especially beneath trees.

Another signal of the need for water is the loss of resilience—the ability of a lawn to bounce back into shape. Take a walk across your lawn. If your footprints remain visible for more than a few seconds, especially in the morning, your lawn needs water.

It is best to soak the soil deeply and then not water again until the top inch or two of soil begins to dry. Allowing the ground to dry partially between waterings allows oxygen to re-enter the soil, where it is needed for proper root growth.

Moisture-testing devices   A reliable way to check for adequate watering is with a soil moisture tester or a soil core sampler. There are two types of moisture testers: mechanical and electrical. The most useful type, called a tensiometer, is a mechanical device that can be attached to an electrical system. It has a porous ceramic cup at the tip, which is coupled to a vacuum gauge at the other end. The cup is kept filled with water. As the soil dries out, water is pulled downward through the cup, causing the gauge to register higher tension in units called centibars (cb). In most soils, a reading in the 70 cb range indicates the need for watering.

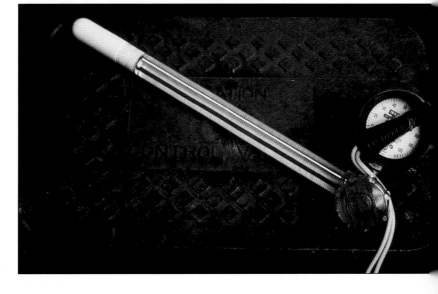

Top: When rainfall needs supplementing, use sprinklers to soak the soil deeply. Bottom: A tensiometer measures moisture in the soil. Attached to an automatic sprinkler system, it can trigger watering as needed.

Making Your Lawn More Drought Resistant

When drought conditions exist, a lawn slows its growth, becomes wilted and brown, and may die. If you live in an area where water conservation is requested or enforced, you simply have to hope that your lawn survives the stress. If it dies, replant it with a more drought-tolerant grass or ground cover, or with drought-tolerant shrubs, when suitable weather returns.

In general, the best way to ensure that your lawn survives a drought is to keep it in good health. The less stress your lawn is under to start with, the less impact the drought will have. Here are other ways to make your lawn more drought resistant:

• Do not apply high-nitrogen fertilizer to a drought-stricken lawn, because this encourages water-consuming leaf growth. Instead, make occasional light applications of fertilizers that are somewhat lower in nitrogen and higher in phosphorus and potassium, such as 10-5-5 or 10-6-4, which stimulate root development. A vigorous root system helps the lawn take up more of the water it receives.

• Increase the lawn's mowing height by about half an inch. For example, if you normally keep your lawn 1½ inches tall, aim for 2 inches. This extra height helps shade the crowns of the plants during hot weather. Never remove more than one third of the leaf blade at a single mowing.

• Pull or spot-spray weeds as they appear. Weeds can thrive in a drought-stressed lawn, looking unsightly and robbing your lawn of water and nutrients. Left unchecked, weeds will crowd out desirable grasses.

• Apply a preemergent herbicide before an anticipated drought period to keep weeds from sprouting in the first place. Preemergent herbicides, of a type intended for use on lawns, are excellent for preventing major weed infestations.

• Have your lawn aerated, if possible, before the drought period begins. Aeration will improve water penetration and encourage deeper roots. Aeration creates numerous small "wells" that keep precious water from running off. When broken up with a rake or lawn mower, the plugs of soil pulled out of the ground during aeration create a light mulch that slows evaporation.

• Have your sprinkler system evaluated. Old or poorly designed sprinkler systems can be very inefficient. Upgrading your existing sprinkler system can save you water and money.

• Watch for extremely wet spots around sprinkler heads. These can signal a leak or a partially broken pipe.

• Water early in the morning. Midday watering can waste water, especially when the weather is hot. Night watering can also save water, but it may promote mildew in humid climates.

• Water your lawn in two short cycles rather than in one long cycle—especially in clay soils, which absorb water slowly. By splitting your watering into two equal intervals about an hour apart, you will reduce runoff and allow water to penetrate more deeply.

• Check with the weather service for local climate information. This should be helpful in tailoring your watering program. Rain gauges are also a useful tool; by knowing how much rain falls, you can tell how much supplemental water you need. Do not be misled by light drizzles that supply little moisture to the soil. However, watering after a light shower can be an effective way of reducing water loss through evaporation.

Placement of the tensiometer is important. It is best to place the device in a representative area of the lawn, or in the spot that tends to dry out first. Place the tip of the tensiometer at approximately the same depth as the roots of the grass. Once installed, the tensiometer is normally left in place and can be checked just before each watering.

Portable tensiometers are also available. These are useful for checking parts of the lawn that are growing under vastly different conditions. They can be used to measure the moisture around shrubs, trees, or container plants.

If you have an automatically controlled sprinkler system, you can buy an automatic type of tensiometer that is used with the system's timer to turn water on and off. The sprinkler comes on only when the soil moisture falls below the level you have set. The system's timer then takes over and turns off the sprinklers after a preset interval.

Tensiometers and other types of moisture sensors can be found at irrigation supply stores and in some garden supply catalogs. Be sure to follow the installation directions carefully, and check the device often to make sure it is functioning correctly.

If you are using a soil core sampler (a metal tube that is pushed into the ground to extract a soil sample), insert it 6 to 12 inches into the soil. You will pull out a cross section of soil that you can check for moisture content, along with anything else that might be happening underground—including root development and root depth. The tube should be pushed into the soil approximately twenty-four hours after watering, when the soil is neither bone dry nor extremely muddy.

If the core is moist to a depth of only 2 to 3 inches, then the lawn needs to be watered longer so that roots can grow to their full potential depth. This is at least 6 to 12 inches for most grass types. It is best to test the soil in several locations to see how deeply the water is penetrating in different areas of the lawn. Soil core samplers are most often found at irrigation and scientific supply stores.

Another way to test for soil moisture is to poke the lawn in several places with a screwdriver. The lawn has received an adequate amount of water if the tool easily penetrates 6 to 12 inches of soil.

How Long to Water? Let Your Water Meter Tell You

Your water meter measures water in cubic feet. It can accurately gauge how much water you have applied in a set amount of time.

Use the following conversion factors to figure out how long to leave the sprinklers on.

• To cover 1,000 square feet with an inch of water takes 624 gallons.

• 7.48 gallons = one cubic foot.

• 83 cubic feet of water covers 1,000 square feet, 1 inch deep.

Judging watering frequency How long your lawn can go between waterings depends on several factors: what kind of grass and soil you have, what the weather is like, and what pattern of watering you have established.

By and large, most warm-season grasses can exist on less water than cool-season grasses, but even cultivars of a single grass species may range widely in their watering requirements. The Lawn Grass Comparisons chart on page 21 compares the characteristics of different grass types. The descriptions of grasses beginning on page 11 may also help you determine how often to water your type of grass.

Local weather tempers the amount of water a lawn needs. The water requirements for a given lawn can range from a minimum of $\frac{1}{10}$ inch per day in cool, still, shady conditions, to a maximum of ½ inch per day in times of full sun, hot temperature, high wind, and low humidity. Obviously, the hotter and drier it is, the more frequently you will need to water.

Soil conditions also affect how often you need to water. In sandy soils, an inch of water applied to the surface will soak down quickly to about 12 inches, but will need frequent replenishing, usually once a week. In loam soil, this distance is 8 inches. In clay soil, the water will soak down only 5 inches but will remain in the soil longer, usually 10 to 14 days.

Finally, the frequency at which you water your lawn sets up its own self-perpetuating pattern. Roots grow only where there is water, so if you consistently wet only the top few inches of soil, the roots do not venture deeper. Eventually, the limited size of the root system forces you into watering more often. That means trouble, because frequent watering keeps the surface wet, which is ideal for weeds and diseases. If roots go deep into the soil, they can draw on a larger underground water supply and the lawn can go much longer between waterings.

How Much to Water

Many people think that more watering is better, since extra water will simply drain away. However, this is not the case. Too much watering can quickly leach fertilizers and nutrients from around the root zone, and can make the grass grow faster and need more frequent mowing. Constant moisture can also promote weed growth and diseases.

On the other hand, if a lawn is not watered enough, its roots will remain shallow and thus unable to make use of water that penetrates farther into the soil. The lawn will thus be more susceptible to stresses caused by insects, diseases, and unusual fluctuations in temperature and rainfall.

To keep grass roots growing deeply, it is important to moisten the soil to a depth of 6 to 12 inches. Water penetrates less deeply in fine-textured soils and more deeply in coarser soils, so the precise amount will vary with the soil type. You need not apply this water all at once. For most soils and lawns, it is better to divide the application into two or three installments. Doing this prevents wasteful runoff by allowing the water to soak in more slowly.

To determine whether the water has gone down far enough, wait 24 hours after watering and then check the soil moisture with a coring tube or screwdriver. If it penetrates 6 to 12 inches of soil without much resistance, the lawn is wet enough. You can also use a tensiometer to test this.

Apply water as uniformly as possible and no faster than the soil can absorb it. Clay soils tend to absorb water more slowly than loam or sandy soils. Avoid applying so much at one time that it results in wasteful runoff. If runoff occurs, divide the watering into timed intervals. Sprinkle until the soil cannot take anymore, then stop for 20 to 30 minutes to allow for absorption. Continue watering until the desired amount has been applied.

When to Water

Some people say that early morning is the best time to water. Others swear by afternoon or evening watering. Although each time has its advantages, morning is generally best.

During the afternoon, evaporation caused by wind and sun is at a maximum, which means that less of the water applied actually reaches the lawn. Wind can disrupt sprinkler patterns, causing poor coverage. Local water consumption is usually highest in the afternoon, which can result in low water pressure. Keep in mind, too, that drought symptoms are more evident in the afternoon and evening. These symptoms can be induced by the higher temperatures and winds typical of that time of day, but are not always an indication of water stress. Often the grass regains its bright green color as temperatures and winds subside.

In spite of these disadvantages, syringing (light watering) in the afternoon can benefit your lawn on hot days. When temperatures reach their highest during the day, alleviate the heat stress of your lawn by wetting it just enough to moisten and cool the grass blades.

Most lawns become wet at night naturally by the dew, but you may still water in the evening. In some areas, leaving a water-soaked lawn overnight may promote disease. However, proper fertilizing, regular dethatching and aerating, and mowing at recommended heights do more to prevent disease than switching from evening waterings to a different time of day.

All things considered, early morning is usually the ideal time to water. Morning waterings usually take advantage of less wind, milder temperatures, and adequate water pressure. Unlike afternoon watering, morning watering gives the water time to soak down to the roots without evaporating.

These are only guidelines. The best rule is: Water when the lawn needs it.

Watering New Lawns

A special set of rules applies for watering newly seeded or sodded lawns. Sprinkling is, at the least, an everyday requirement. For seeds to germinate or sod roots to knit, watering is often required more than once a day so that the soil does not dry out during the rooting period. For more on watering newly seeded lawns, see page 38; for newly planted sprigs and plugs, see pages 40 and 41. For new sod lawns, see page 45.

PORTABLE SPRINKLERS

Understanding your lawn's watering require-ments will do you no good unless you have a reliable way of meeting them. Portable sprin-klers, consisting of a garden hose with a remov-able sprinkler head attached at one end, are a simple and inexpensive way to apply water to a lawn. Although less precise and efficient than automatic underground systems, they get the job done. If you have a small lawn, or if you live where supplemental watering is required only occasionally, they may be all you need.

If you decide to water with a portable sprin-kler, choose one that will provide uniform cov-erage with minimum waste. Many kinds of portable sprinklers are available, with many patterns of water distribution. The following are some guidelines to help you evaluate and compare them.

The Container Test

Measuring the water distribution of a sprinkler is quite easy. Set up a gridlike pattern of small containers of the same size on a section of the lawn, extending them at set intervals from close to the sprinkler head to just at the edges of where the water reaches. Turn the sprinkler on at the normal operating pressure; leave it on for a set period of time, then record the amount of water deposited in each container. This gives you a good idea of the sprinkler pattern, as well as the amount of water distributed through the area it covers.

Depending on the type of grass and soil you have (an inch of water penetrates about 12 inches in sand, about 8 inches in loam, and about 5 inches in clay soil), you can use the container test as an easy way to determine how long to keep the sprinkler on. You can also use it to gauge how much to overlap sprinkling patterns.

Types of Portable Sprinklers

There are many types of portable sprinklers, each with its own pattern of water delivery. There are four common varieties: stationary, oscillating arm, whirling head, and impulse. When shopping for a portable sprinkler, choose the one that will most efficiently cover the area where it is to be used.

Use the container test to check the distribution pattern of a sprinkler.

Left: A stationary sprinkler is best for spot watering. Right: An oscillating-arm sprinkler covers a rectangular area.

Left: A whirling-head sprinkler may give uneven coverage unless watering areas are overlapped. Right: An impulse sprinkler waters evenly, and its spray volume can be adjusted.

Stationary sprinklers consist of a small metal or plastic chamber pierced with holes that spray water in a fixed pattern. These types of sprinklers deliver water to different parts of the lawn at different rates, depending on the arrangement of holes. The rates may vary from 8 inches an hour in one spot, to 2 inches an hour just 4 feet away, to almost nothing near the sprinkler head. There is no easily predictable pattern in which to place these sprinklers for uniform overlapping. However, it is unfair to label these types of sprinklers "useless." As long as you know how they distribute water, you can use them for spot watering or for supplementing other types of sprinklers. Variants of stationary sprinklers called cone sprayers have a single or double large hole instead of pinholes. They are best for small areas.

Oscillating-arm sprinklers have an arched, perforated pipe that sweeps back and forth to deliver water in a rectangular pattern. Older models used to be faulted for depositing most of their water near the sprinkler head and sending decreasing amounts toward the periphery. Newer versions have solved this problem by stalling momentarily when the arm is farthest from its upright position. This allows more water to reach the outer boundaries.

The whirling-head sprinkler has two or more rotating arms that spray jets of water in a circular pattern. The amount of water delivered decreases with the distance from the source of the spray, with most water falling between 4 and 8 feet out. Water distribution is uneven when this sprinkler is used without a system of overlapping. With a 50 percent overlap, however, efficiency increases and the sprinkler becomes quite useful.

Impulse (or impact) sprinklers are best for large areas and are commonly used on golf courses and in parks. An internal jet rotates the sprinkler, which delivers pulses of water in a part circle to a full circle. The head can be adjusted to send out a strong jet, a gentle mist, or anything in between. Coverage to the lawn is usually quite even.

Be aware that different brands of the same type of sprinkler may distribute water in very different patterns. Without knowing this, a conscientious waterer can end up with sections of lawn that are either overwatered or underwatered. This produces uneven green and brown areas and unnecessary weeds and disease. Along with knowing about soil, climate, and wind conditions, you should be aware of how your sprinkler distributes water.

UNDERGROUND SPRINKLER SYSTEMS

An underground system has many advantages over a portable sprinkler; the most obvious is the convenience of not having to constantly move it. Most underground systems are also more efficient than portable types. Sprinkler heads apply predictable amounts of water over an exact area, eliminating the most serious deficiency of portable sprinklers: uneven water distribution. An underground system combined with an automatic timer or moisture sensor can water even while you are away from home.

If you are planting a new lawn or reseeding an existing one, now is the time to consider installing an underground system. It is possible to add a system to an area that is already landscaped, but it is harder to do and your lawn will need repairing when you are finished.

Before deciding to put in an underground system, weigh the effort and cost involved. Companies specializing in irrigation can often install a system within a few days. Doing it yourself may take several weekends, and in the meantime your lawn will be cluttered with equipment and materials. Installing your own system also requires some skill with tools. However, if you are willing to do the work yourself,

you can save a great deal of money. Many manufacturers now provide illustrated, step-by-step instructions with their systems, making them easier than ever to design and install. Irrigation supply stores and some hardware and home improvement stores employ specialists who can give you further guidance. If you buy all your materials from a single irrigation supply store, the store may design the sprinkler system for you.

Preparing for a System

When you have determined who will be doing the work, be sure to choose both the system manufacturer and the supplier carefully. Consult neighbors who have underground systems;

Top: An underground sprinkler system should be designed for "head-to-head" coverage, so that spray from each sprinkler head lands on adjoining heads. Bottom: Sprinkler heads with less than full-circle coverage are used to direct the flow of water where it is needed. Half-circle and quarter-circle heads are the most common types.

A Multi-Circuit Sprinkler System: Layout and Components

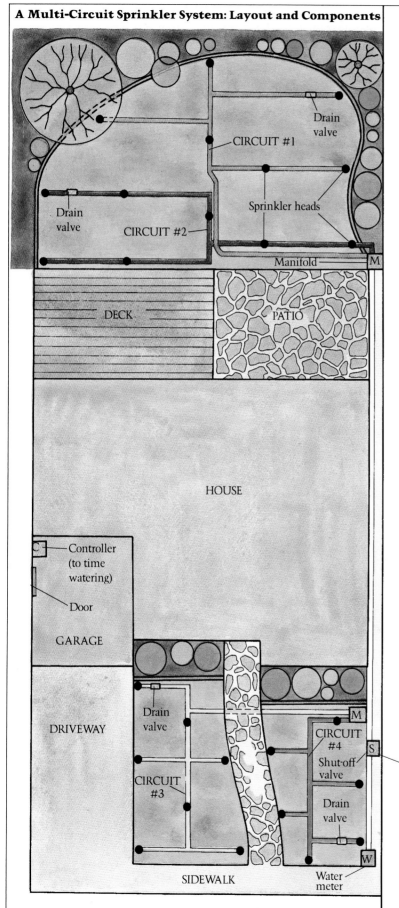

Drain valve

CIRCUIT #1

Sprinkler heads

Drain valve

CIRCUIT #2

Manifold — M

DECK

PATIO

HOUSE

C — Controller (to time watering)

Door

GARAGE

DRIVEWAY

Drain valve

CIRCUIT #3

Drain valve

M

CIRCUIT #4

S

Shut-off valve

Drain valve

W

SIDEWALK

Water meter

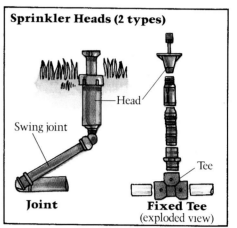

Sprinkler Heads (2 types)

Head

Swing joint

Tee

Joint

Fixed Tee
(exploded view)

Manifold

Control valves

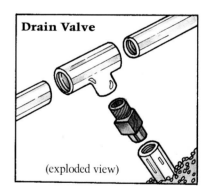

Drain Valve

(exploded view)

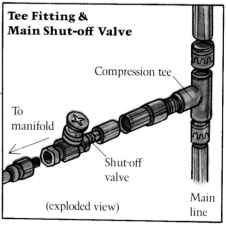

Tee Fitting & Main Shut-off Valve

Compression tee

To manifold

Shut-off valve

(exploded view)

Main line

also talk to irrigation specialists, nursery owners, or a local landscape contractor for advice about the brands and models that will best suit your needs. Then either write to the manufacturer or see your local distributor for detailed information. If you are installing the system yourself, read the installation instructions before purchasing the system, to make sure they are easy to follow.

Before visiting an irrigation specialist or ordering supplies, use a measuring tape and graph paper to make a scale drawing of your lawn and its surroundings. Show the location of the water supply and any shrubs, trees, paved areas, fences, mailboxes, raised planters, buried drainage or power lines, and other features that could affect the sprinkler design and installation. Also note the prevailing wind direction and sun and shade areas, as well as high and low spots in your landscape. Indicate any water-sensitive or especially thirsty plants that will need to be watered by a separate line.

If you have an idea of how the system might be laid out, draw in the approximate locations of the sprinkler heads, marking colored circles around those that are to be on the same circuit.

Next, draw the pipe going from the house water supply to the manifold—the control unit of the sprinkler system. Composed of a group of control valves, the manifold regulates the flow of water from the source to each individual circuit. From the manifold, draw in the pipelines for each circuit. Plan to use the same trench for installing two or more water lines wherever possible. If you can, avoid going under walks or driveways or near trees. The illustration on the opposite page shows the layout of a typical system.

Once you have made a detailed plan, measure the flow rate of your household water system. The flow rate is determined by the available water pressure, which must be great enough to supply ample water to all sprinklers in a line. The easiest way to determine the flow rate is to measure the available gallons per minute, or GPM. You do this by measuring how many seconds it takes an outdoor faucet, turned wide open, to fill a container of a given size, and then converting the result to gallons per minute. For example, if a 5-gallon bucket fills in 25 seconds, you would divide 5 gallons by 25 seconds to determine that the flow rate is $\frac{1}{5}$ (.2) gallon per second. You would then multiply this by 60 seconds to determine that the flow rate is 12 GPM.

The flow rate, along with your scale drawing, helps the irrigation specialist design your system and specify parts for it, including the length, diameter, and number of lines; the number and capacity of nozzles on each line; and the watering pattern of each nozzle or other outlet. Even if you are designing and installing the system on your own, you can avoid costly problems by having your plan checked by a professional.

MOWING

Many people underestimate the importance of mowing. A lawn that is mowed to the right height at the right time resists weeds, insects, and disease, and appears lush and healthy. Infrequent mowing often results in the removal of too much grass at one time, and eventually produces a lawn that looks thin, spotty, or burned. On the other hand, grass can also be weakened by mowing too frequently, especially if it is kept short.

How Often to Mow

How often your lawn needs mowing depends on several things: how often and how much you water and fertilize, what time of year it is, and the type of grass in your lawn.

The fertilizer you apply affects the growth rate of your lawn, and consequently the frequency of mowing. Lawns receiving fertilizer that is very high in nitrogen often require more frequent mowing.

Cool-season and warm-season grasses respond differently to seasonal temperature changes. When cool-season grasses slow down or become dormant during summer heat, mowing may only be necessary once every two or three weeks. However, during spring and fall, cool-season grasses grow more vigorously and usually need mowing at least once a week. Warm-season grasses grow very little if at all in winter, and slowly in spring and fall. Mowing is infrequent during these times. During the hot days of summer, however, growth is vigorous and mowing should be more frequent.

During periods of vigorous lawn growth, most people find it convenient to mow their lawns on a weekly schedule, such as every Saturday morning. Unfortunately, this is not appropriate for all lawn grasses. Even though you can establish a general schedule for both cool-season and warm-season grasses, different types of grass still grow at different rates. For example, although common bermudagrass may do well when mowed once a week during mid-summer, well-fertilized hybrid bermudagrass may need to be mowed every two or three days. If you can, match your mowing schedule to the growth rate of the grass.

The Right Height

Proper mowing height depends primarily on the type of grass. The chart on page 61 recommends mowing heights for the major lawn grasses. The rule of thumb is to mow when the grass grows from one-fourth to one-third taller than its recommended mowing height. For example, if you normally mow for your lawn at 2 inches, mow when it is about 3 inches high.

The penalty for not paying attention to the recommended mowing height is a stiff one. By letting grass grow too high and then cutting away half or more at one time, you expose stems that have been shaded and may burn in strong sunlight. If the lawn is yellowish after you mow, you have waited too long. The grass will recover and grow back, but more important, roots are severely shocked by heavy mowing and may need several weeks to recover.

The cutting height of a rotary mower is adjusted by raising or lowering its wheels. To keep your lawn healthy, cut it at the proper height for your grass.

Research has shown a direct relationship between the height of the cut and the depth of roots. When grass is properly mowed to its recommended height, roots grow deeper. In turn, a deep root system makes lawn care much easier because the lawn is in overall better condition and health.

Grasses tend to spread either horizontally or vertically. For instance, bentgrass and bermudagrass spread horizontally by creeping rhizomes and stolons. Because these stems parallel the ground as well as the cut of the mower, they are not normally mowed off. Unless these grasses are mowed low, preferably with a heavy reel mower, they will have problems with thatch.

For the most part, warm-season grasses can tolerate closer mowing than cool-season grasses. If cool-season varieties are mowed too low (at 1 inch or less), they usually begin to produce roots less vigorously, lose their deep green color, and show signs of thinning.

At low cutting heights, diseases such as dollar spot, leaf spot, and rust are more of a problem because they can envelop the whole plant more quickly. Grass that is allowed to grow to its recommended height not only resists diseases better, but also helps shade and cool the surface of the soil, preventing many weeds from germinating.

Warm-season and cool-season grasses growing primarily in the shade should be allowed to grow approximately ½ inch higher than the midpoint of their recommended cutting range. This provides more leaf surface for the food-producing process of photosynthesis.

In general, lawns going into winter should be cut at the midpoint of their cutting range or somewhat shorter, rather than left long during the winter. This prevents the grass from matting and the excess leaf blade tissue from decaying. If given this final mowing, the lawn will have better color during the winter (in mild climates) and will green up sooner in the spring.

Mowing New Lawns

Newly planted lawns are more delicate than established ones, and you need to be more careful when mowing them. The soil is soft and the young grass plants usually are not deeply rooted by the first mowing. On the other hand, mowing young lawns, especially those planted vegetatively with plugs or sprigs, encourages the plants to spread, thus promoting a thicker lawn.

Mowing Heights

The following are recommended mowing heights for the most popular lawn grasses. In most areas and situations, a lawn will look good when mowed at any height within the range for its grass type.

Grass	Height in Inches	Grass	Height in Inches
Cool-Season Grasses		**Warm-Season Grasses**	
Bentgrass, Creeping	¼–¾	Bahiagrass	2–3
Bluegrass, Kentucky	1½–2½	Bermudagrass, Common	¾–1½
Bluegrass, Rough	1½–2	Bermudagrass, Hybrid	½–1
Fescue, Chewings	1–2½	Centipedegrass	1–2
Fescue, Dwarf	1½–2½	St. Augustine Grass	1½–2½
Fescue, Hard	1–2½	Zoysiagrass	1–2
Fescue, Red	1½–2½		
Fescue, Tall	2–3	**Native Grasses**	
Ryegrass, Annual	1½–2	Blue Grama	2–3
Ryegrass, Perennial	1½–2	Buffalograss	2½–3
		Smooth Brome	3–6

Mow any new lawn for the first time after it has grown a third higher than the regular mowing height. For example, a lawn that should be maintained at a 2-inch height should be mowed when it reaches 3 inches. If possible, do not remove more than a third of the total height of the grass—in this case, 1 inch.

If you can, use a mower that is not too heavy, especially if the soil is still soft. A lightweight rotary or a push-type reel mower is your best bet. Make sure the mower blades are sharp; the young grass plants can be easily pulled from the soil by dull blades.

If the soil remains too soft or if the new grass is too loosely knit to mow without damage, it is best to wait. Let the lawn continue to grow, then lower the cut gradually until it is down to the proper height. Reduce the cutting height by ½ inch every second mowing until you reach the recommended mowing height.

Grass Clippings

Whether to leave clippings on a lawn or to pick them up is a question many gardeners ask. There are advantages and disadvantages to leaving grass clippings on your lawn, depending on the type of grass you have and how well you maintain it.

Leaving finely cut clippings of cool-season grasses on the lawn does not usually cause or contribute to thatch. It is the woody, slow-to-decompose stems of warm-season grass blades that normally contribute most to thatch buildup.

Finely cut clippings return nutrients and other beneficial materials to the lawn, as they contain approximately 75 to 80 percent water, 3 to 6 percent nitrogen, 1 percent phosphorus, and 1 to 3 percent potassium. The nitrogen component of grass clippings can provide about one third of the yearly nitrogen requirement of a lawn. Other nutrients such as calcium may also be contained in the clippings. As they decompose they fertilize the lawn naturally. Leaving finely cut grass clippings on the lawn surface can also be a time-saver. If you normally rake up grass clippings after you mow, simply leaving them in place can reduce your mowing-and-raking time by about a third.

At certain times, however, it makes sense to remove clippings from your lawn. First, clippings can be unsightly. They are removed from many intensely maintained lawns for just this reason. Second, if you do not mow your lawn frequently, you will be cutting off longer lengths of grass that can mat down and block light from the lawn. These heavy clippings may weaken or smother the grass, add to thatch buildup, and spread disease organisms. It is best to remove enough of these clippings that only a light cover remains.

Some people remove clippings to use as a compost or mulch in a vegetable garden. This trend is growing, as more and more communities outlaw the depositing of grass clippings in household trash. Watch for weeds in the clippings, though; if their seeds germinate, they

A mulching mower chops up clippings so fine that they sink invisibly into the lawn, saving cleanup time and returning nutrients to the grass.

can create havoc in your garden. Also make sure that potential composting materials do not contain broadleaf herbicides, which can harm your garden plants.

To remove clippings from your lawn, use a steel-tine lawn rake after mowing. The tines are made of spring steel, and snap back into position even when bent backward. A plastic or bamboo lawn rake can also be used. An easier solution is to purchase a catch bag for your lawn mower.

LAWN MOWERS

Almost every homeowner with a lawn has a lawn mower, and the number of varieties and styles of these grows each year. The two most common types are the reel and the rotary. Each type has several variations, including manual, gas, or electric, and hand pushed, self-propelled, or riding. Most have some kind of bagging attachment or grass catcher.

It pays to look around for the type that best fits your needs, and to buy the highest-quality mower you can afford. A good mower should provide you with years of reliable service. Also look for equipment that is large and powerful enough for the job. The money you save by

buying a smaller, cheaper machine may be insignificant when weighed against the extra time it takes to mow a lawn. For example, it would take at least 2½ hours (and a 5½-mile walk) to cut a 1-acre lawn using a walk-behind mower with an 18-inch cutting width. A riding mower with a 36-inch cutting width could mow it in about 30 minutes.

Before buying a lawn mower, look it over carefully. Consider its starting system, maneuverability, and features for adjusting handle height and cutting height. Make sure the grass catcher is easy to put on and take off, and ask about the safety features.

Mowers can be specialized. Some are designed to cut high weeds, while others are engineered to produce the carpetlike nap of a putting green. However, most of these are inappropriate for home lawns.

Rotary Mowers

The power rotary mower is the most popular model, having long since replaced the reel mower as the standard for home lawns. Powered by gas or electricity, this type of mower is generally less expensive, more versatile, and easier to handle and maintain. It withstands

Lawn Mowers

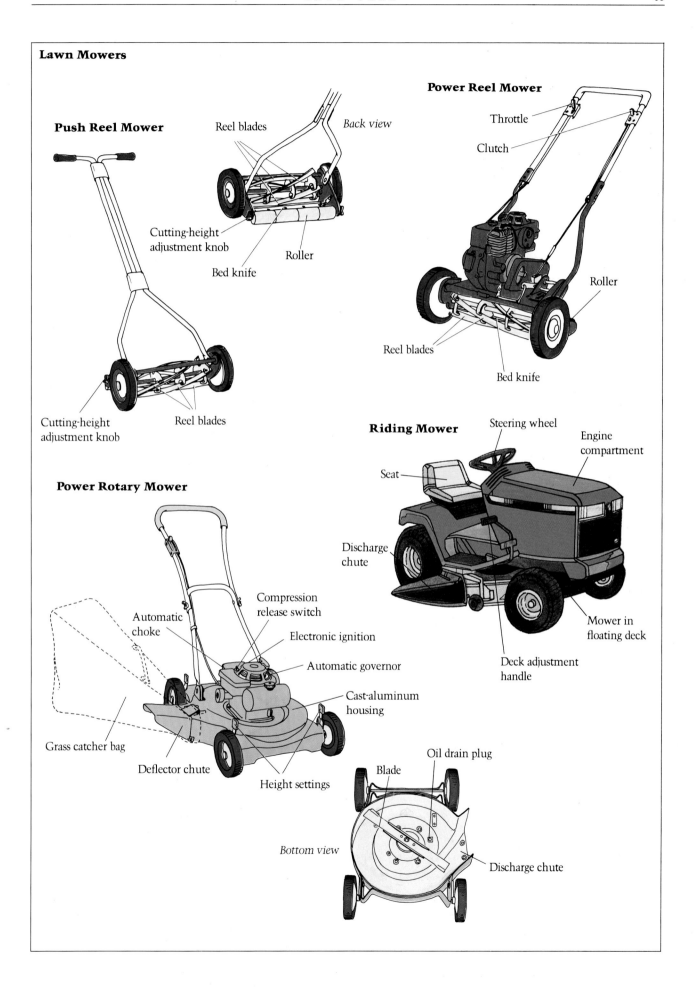

Power Reel Mower

Throttle

Clutch

Roller

Reel blades

Bed knife

Push Reel Mower

Reel blades

Back view

Cutting-height
adjustment knob

Roller

Bed knife

Cutting-height
adjustment knob

Reel blades

Power Rotary Mower

Compression
release switch

Automatic
choke

Electronic ignition

Automatic governor

Cast-aluminum
housing

Grass catcher bag

Deflector chute

Height settings

Riding Mower

Steering wheel

Engine
compartment

Seat

Discharge
chute

Mower in
floating deck

Deck adjustment
handle

Oil drain plug

Blade

Bottom view

Discharge chute

rougher use as well. Its blades cut like a spinning scythe, which surpasses a reel for taller growing, less intensively maintained lawns. The blades are also easier to sharpen.

However, power rotary mowers require greater caution in use. They need larger motors with more horsepower; they do not cut as cleanly as a properly sharpened reel mower; and few can mow lower than 1 inch. The mower also shakes if its blades go out of balance.

Rotary mowers come in hand-pushed and self-propelled models. The hand-pushed type has been the most popular for decades and has serviced many a lawn. The more expensive self-propelled type normally has various speed adjustments and a handle that acts as an accelerator, making the mower much easier to use.

If your lawn is very large, you probably need a riding mower, which conserves both energy and time. Riding mowers come in rotary and reel models, but rotaries are the most common types. Although they are enjoyable for adults to drive, riding mowers are expensive, need a good-sized storage area, and require skilled operation and maintenance.

Reel Mowers

Although now eclipsed in popularity by rotary power mowers, reel mowers are still preferred for fine lawns because they conform better to land contours and because their scissors action produces a cleaner cut. They are especially useful for bentgrass and bermudagrass lawns because they can be adjusted to cut quite low. However, they are impractical on rough, uneven ground or for tall grasses with high, wiry seed heads.

Reel mowers are available in manual models or models powered by gasoline or electricity. Power reel mowers discharge clippings from either the rear (rear-throw mowers) or the front (front-throw mowers). The rear-throw type is more widely available and less expensive.

Front-throw reel mowers are used primarily by professional landscape gardeners. They are usually well made and can stand constant use. The weight and power of these mowers makes them perfect for the low-mowing requirements of bentgrass, bermudagrass, and zoysiagrass lawns. Height is also fairly easy to adjust on these, usually with a lever.

Mowing Hints

Here are some tips to help you mow your lawn more safely and effectively.

• Mow at the proper cutting height for your lawn (see the Mowing Heights chart on page 61). Adjust a reel mower by raising or lowering the roller with its knobs, screws, or lever. You can check the cutting height by measuring the distance between the bed knife and a hard surface. Adjust a rotary mower by raising or lowering its wheels. Some rotary mower blades are at the same level as the lower edge of the blade housing, so you can easily check the cutting height by measuring the skirt's height above a hard surface. If that does not give the correct figure, you can simply cut a small section of lawn and measure its height with a ruler.

• Start the mower on a level surface. Before starting a walk-behind rotary mower, put one foot firmly atop the mower deck and the other foot on solid ground at a safe distance from the mower and its blades.

• Always push a rotary mower forward. If you pull it backward, there is too great a risk that you could pull it over your foot.

• If grass is coming out from a side chute, make certain that no one is within range of stones or other objects that may be ejected with it. Before reaching in to remove clogged grass, turn off the power and disconnect the ignition wire from the spark plug. If the mower has a catch bag, shut off the power before removing and emptying it.

• Do not cut wet grass. It mows unevenly, the clippings are messy, and they can mat and block light from the grass. There is also the danger of slipping on wet slopes.

• Vary mowing patterns. Mowing in the same direction every time tends to compact the soil and create wear patterns. Grass tends to lean or grow in the direction in which it is mowed, so altering the mowing pattern will keep it straighter. For a checkerboard effect, make a second pass over the lawn at right angles to the first.

• Mow slight slopes at a slight diagonal. If there is a chance of slippage on a steeper slope, tie a rope to the mower and mow downward from the top. Or better yet, plant a ground cover that does not need mowing.

• If the ground is uneven in some areas because the soil has settled, be careful not to scalp the high spots. Either mow the whole lawn higher or regrade it.

• Sharp turns with a mower can cause uneven cutting. Make wide turns or take advantage of sidewalks and driveways, but be aware of rocks or debris on paved surfaces.

• If you are using a reel mower, you can give the lawn an attractive checkered finish by mowing it a second time at right angles to the first.

• If your mower is loud, wear earplugs to protect your hearing.

• Always stop the engine before leaving the mower, if only for a minute. An unattended mower can run away down a slope or endanger a child.

Other Mowers

Electric nylon mowers cut grass with nearly the same efficiency as steel-bladed mowers and are much safer. Two counter-rotating disks powered by separate electric motors spin monofilament line to mow and trim your lawn. They are best for light cutting.

Mulching mowers are rotary mowers designed to cut leaf tissue into pieces that are small enough to fall into the turf rather than remain on top of the grass. The clippings tend to decompose quickly because of their small size. Mulching mowers either lack a discharge chute or have a chute that can be closed. The clippings are trapped beneath the mowing deck in the cutting chamber and are recut until they are finely chopped. Mulching mowers do not work very well when the grass is wet or if the grass clippings are very long.

Several other less common types of mowers are available for special jobs. Flail mowers, also known as hammer-knife mowers, use loose, T-shaped blades revolving on a horizontal shaft to cut grass. They are useful in maintaining rough areas such as vacant lots and the sides of highways. Sickle bar mowers are perfect for an empty lot overgrown with weeds. They are the same sort of mower that farmers use to cut field oats and other hays and grains. Heavy reel mowers are useful for the one or two times you need to cut the lawn extra low for thatch removal. High-wheel rotary mowers cut higher than most rotary mowers—about 4 inches—and are easy to maneuver over rough terrain and around plants and edges.

MOWER MAINTENANCE

Taking care of your lawn mower will lengthen its life as well as eliminate time-consuming problems. The manufacturer's maintenance manual is the best guide to help you keep your mower in good working order.

Keep the mower blades sharp. You can tell that blades need sharpening when the cut ends of grass blades look ragged. The blades of rotary mowers are easy to sharpen at home. Only a small portion at the end of the blade actually cuts the grass, so this job is easier than it seems. First, take out the blade by removing the nut that secures it. (It is best to remove the mower's spark plug wire beforehand, to prevent the mower from starting accidentally.) Sharpen the edge of the blade with a file or

grindstone, making sure to even out any rough spots. Check the balance by spinning the blade on a spare bolt, inserted in its center hole, to see if the blade rotates evenly. If it doesn't, take the blade to a garden equipment shop, which can balance it for a reasonable fee.

Blades of reel mowers are tricky to remove and sharpen because of their curved shape. Take any mower to a shop if you have doubts about sharpening its blades.

Gasoline-powered mowers have additional maintenance needs. Be sure the motor oil is at the correct level. Use the proper type of gasoline and keep the spark plug connection clean. Clean the mower blades after use with a soft spray of water. Forceful cleaning with water or air can push dirt into delicate bearings. Do not spray water onto a hot engine. Keep gaskets and fittings tight, as gas or oil leaks can kill grass.

To help prevent rust and corrosion, it is best to keep your mower covered or out of the elements when it is not in use. Keep the exterior parts of the deck and handle clean and dirt free. Clean out grass that may accumulate under the mower around the edges of the cutting blades.

If you store your mower over the winter, clean it and drain the gas tank. In spring, change the oil, clean the spark plug, clean or replace the fuel filter, and refill the gas tank.

EDGING AND TRIMMING

No matter what type of lawn mower you use, it will inevitably miss a few stray blades of grass in hard-to-reach areas. Trimming (cutting stray high grasses) and edging (grooming the lawn's edges by cutting along them vertically) give the lawn a finished look.

A number of tools make edging and trimming easier. Hand-operated grass shears, which work like scissors, are useful for trimming and even edging small lawns. Long-handled grass shears are better than short-handled ones because they allow you to stand up as you cut. A manually operated edger is better for the edging operation because it is specialized to cut vertically. There are two manual types: a turf edger, which consists of a semicircular blade at the end of a long handle, and a rotary edger, whose star-shaped cutting wheel is attached to a plastic or rubber guide wheel, also at the end of a long handle.

If your lawn is large or has many edges, you may want to purchase a power trimmer or

Left: An electric string trimmer cuts stray weeds or grass blades that the lawn mower has missed.
Right: A gas-powered edger can be a timesaver for very large lawns. The sidewalk guides it in a straight line.

edger. Power trimmers are available in various models that run on gasoline or electricity. The most common type, the string trimmer, cuts with a rapidly whirling nylon filament that rotates at the end of a long handle. The handle is usually curved to allow the string to cut at a more convenient angle. In addition to trimming along the edges of a lawn, this device is useful for cutting patches of tall weeds and grasses. Be sure to wear goggles when using this type of trimmer so that your eyes are protected against flying debris.

Gas-powered trimmers with reciprocating blades are somewhat safer to use than string trimmers because they eject less debris, and because the blades stop as soon as the engine is turned off. Like string trimmers, they are easy to handle and are fairly lightweight.

Power edgers are run by electricity or gasoline. Electric edgers are motorized versions of the manually operated rotary type. Gas-powered edgers contain a narrow cutting blade that is rotated rapidly by an engine.

Although most people think of edging and trimming as after-mowing operations, many lawn care professionals actually perform these tasks first. When they save mowing for last, the lawn clippings generated by edging and trimming are picked up by the mower as it collects the clippings in its catch bag or chops them finely to leave on the lawn. This makes for less grass to sweep or blow from walkways and edgings.

It is important to use power trimmers carefully around trees and other plants. Trees can be killed or severely damaged if the cambium layer just under the bark is injured. To shield small lawn trees against damage, wrap a trunk protector around the base of each tree. Available at many nurseries, trunk protectors are rectangles of heavy-duty perforated plastic that have been prerolled to stay in place around a trunk.

Power edgers can damage wood and concrete edgings—or be damaged by them—if not used with care. When working along a concrete edging, try to minimize contact between the tool and the concrete surface, as this quickly wears down the blade. Despite the precautions they require, edgings make the task of edging easier by providing a smooth, straight surface along which to guide tools.

FERTILIZING

Lawn grasses live in an unnatural environment. The grass plants are crowded together and compete with each other—as well as with neighboring trees and shrubs—for water and nutrients. They are mowed regularly, which is highly irregular in nature, and their clippings, a source of nutrients, are often removed.

Because of this competition and the unnatural demands placed on lawns, they must be fertilized. When properly fertilized, a lawn maintains good color, density, and vigor, and it does not easily succumb to insects, weeds, or diseases. When underfertilized, the lawn is not only less attractive, but is also much more susceptible to environmental stresses such as drought.

High-nitrogen fertilizers such as 21-0-0 stimulate top growth, while those higher in phosphorus and potassium such as 15-5-10 encourage root growth, cell division, and disease resistance. A lawn will have best overall health and vigor if given a complete fertilizer (containing nitrogen, phosphorus, and potassium) at least twice a year, preferably in spring and fall—or more often if you are maintaining your lawn intensively. Additional iron, applied if needed, helps give the lawn a dark green color.

The Nutrients a Lawn Needs

Sixteen chemical elements are essential to the growth of lawns. Three of these—carbon, hydrogen, and oxygen—are readily available from air and water, so supplementing them is never necessary. Others, such as nitrogen, may be plentiful in the environment but exist in a form that plants cannot use. Still others are present in smaller quantities that plants eventually deplete.

Nitrogen, phosphorus, and potassium are known as primary nutrients because they must be supplemented in the greatest quantities. The percentage of each of these is listed on fertilizer labels.

Calcium, magnesium, and sulfur are called secondary nutrients because they are needed in lesser amounts. They are often supplied by the soil amendments that are used to adjust pH.

Micronutrients, or trace elements, are needed in very small quantities. They are boron, chlorine, copper, iron, manganese, molybdenum, and zinc. With the exception of iron, these elements rarely need supplementing.

Nitrogen This is by far the most important element that a lawn needs. It promotes rapid shoot growth and gives lawns a healthy color. Nitrogen is the element most often in short supply. When sufficient nitrogen is lacking, growth stops and the lawn becomes pale and yellowish. On the other hand, if there is too much nitrogen, thatch and disease may develop, and the lawn may be more susceptible to heat, drought, and cold. Nitrogen is normally supplied in several ways—from decomposing matter in the soil, from natural fertilizers such as manure, or from commercial organic or inorganic compounds.

Phosphorus This nutrient is needed in lesser amounts than nitrogen, but is still essential for the healthy growth of lawn grasses. It stimulates the early formation and strong growth of the roots, which is why new lawns need it at such a high percentage. However, it is not readily flushed from the soil by watering, and it is needed by established lawns in small quantities; moreover, there is usually some phosphorus present in the soil. As a result, complete lawn fertilizers typically contain only a low percentage of phosphorus, usually in the form of phosphoric acid.

Potassium Potassium is the third primary nutrient listed on a fertilizer container. Like nitrogen, it is flushed out by water, but at a slower rate. It strengthens lawn grasses,

Take care to apply fertilizer evenly. The lighter green patches in this lawn mark spots that a spreader has missed.

enabling them to withstand traffic, resist disease, and conserve water. Grass plants need about half as much potassium as nitrogen, but since many soils supply a considerable amount, not much is usually added to fertilizers. The major source of potassium in fertilizers is muriate of potash.

Calcium, magnesium, and sulfur Compared with other plants, lawn grasses require relatively large amounts of these nutrients. Calcium is either present in adequate quantities in the soil or is added through periodic applications of lime. Dolomite (or dolomitic limestone) supplies magnesium as well as calcium. Most soil sulfur reaches a lawn through the air, water, or organic matter. It is also sometimes added in the form of soil sulfur or gypsum (calcium sulfate). For more information on lime and sulfur and their uses on lawns, see page 30.

Micronutrients Even though micronutrients are used by plants in very small quantities, they are just as essential for plant growth as the primary and secondary nutrients. Apply them with caution, since the difference between deficient and toxic levels is often small. A soil test will tell you if these nutrients need supplementing.

Iron is the micronutrient that is most often lacking. If your lawn doesn't become greener with an application of nitrogen, the problem may be a shortage of iron. This is particularly true in areas where soil pH is high. Iron may be present in these soils, but the high alkalinity makes it chemically unavailable to plants.

A Sample Fertilizer Label

Manufacturers must supply the same basic information on all lawn food labels. State laws and agencies that control plant food stipulate the specific information that must appear on a label. Although labels differ, the most important characteristics, described below, are found on every bag of fertilizer sold as lawn food.

In this example, the heading "Lawn Food" is the equivalent of a brand name.

Referred to as the formula grade or the analysis, these three numbers indicate the percentages of nitrogen, phosphorus, and potassium, in that order, of the contents. The percentages indicate that the ratio of this fertilizer is 6 to 1 to 2.

Guaranteed analysis is the manufacturer's warranty that at least the stated analysis by weight is present in the container. The guaranteed analysis is always stated in this order and form.

The percentages of available nitrogen, phosphoric acid, and soluble potash are listed here because their presence is claimed in the formula grade. If a fertilizer contains nitrogen only, such as in the formula 17-0-0, the zero percentages for the absent primary nutrients are not listed here.

The percentages of the sources of nitrogen are not always required, but most manufacturers supply this information. Nitrogen sources have different characteristics, so it is useful to know which ones are used in the fertilizer you buy. The percentage of water-insoluble nitrogen (WIN) shown in the sample indicates that the fertilizer is medium acting.

The primary nutrients in this fertilizer—nitrogen, phosphorus, and potassium—are derived from these basic products.

Many fertilizers have an acid effect on the soil. In order to completely neutralize the acidifying effects of 1 ton of this fertilizer, you would have to add 800 pounds of calcium carbonate (limestone).

Lawn Food 24-4-8

Guaranteed Analysis:
Total Nitrogen (N)..................................24%
   4.1% Ammoniacal Nitrogen
  15.9% Urea Nitrogen
   4.0% Water-Insoluble Nitrogen
Available Phosphoric Acid (P_2O_5).........4%
Soluble Potash (K_2O)..............................8%
  Primary Nutrients from Urea, Ureaform, Ammonium Sulfate, Ammonium Phosphate, and Muriate of Potash
Potential Acidity 800 lbs. Calcium Carbonate Equivalent per ton.
Net Weight 20 lbs.

Types of Fertilizers

A little shopping at a garden center reveals an abundance of lawn fertilizers. You see labels proclaiming "organic," "fast acting," "slow release," and so on. But if they all contain the same basic elements, what is the difference? Here is a general description of these products.

Natural organic fertilizers The term "natural organic" refers to any fertilizer that is made up of dried or composted plant or animal waste. The variety of natural organic fertilizers is endless. There are manures of all kinds, municipal sewage sludge, blood meals, hoof and horn meals, and seed meals. More and more such products are introduced each year.

Most natural organic fertilizers have distinctly beneficial soil-building properties. Overfertilizing is usually not a problem with these fertilizers, since their action is slow. On the negative side, they are often more bulky, heavy, and difficult to handle than other types of fertilizer. They have a low percentage of nitrogen, so it is necessary to apply a much greater quantity at one time. They may also have an unpleasant smell. However, as the popularity of such products increases, these problems are being addressed by fertilizer manufacturers.

Certain drawbacks will probably remain, though. Because soil microbes must digest the organic material in order to release its nutrients, natural organics are much slower acting than soluble synthetic fertilizers. They are also more variable in their effectiveness, since the activity of the microbes that release the nutrients rises and falls with the soil temperature. Thus, nutrients may be unavailable during the cool days of early spring and late fall, when cool-season grasses are growing actively—yet abundant in summer, when cool-season grasses become partially dormant and should not be fertilized heavily.

Soluble synthetic fertilizers A soluble synthetic fertilizer is one that is produced by chemical reaction, whether from organic or inorganic materials. Some fertilizers labeled organic are actually synthetic, because they have been synthesized from organic compounds.

Soluble synthetic fertilizers (sometimes called quick-release fertilizers) are the most common types used on lawns today. Their big advantages are their speed of action and their predictability. Unlike slow-acting natural organic fertilizers, they release their nutrients rapidly into the soil, and grasses turn green soon after they have been applied. And because their action does not depend on microbial activity, soluble synthetic fertilizers become available to the lawn before the soil has warmed thoroughly in spring, helping to speed lawn growth at a critical time. Moreover, because the characteristics of synthetic fertilizers are known precisely, their effects are easy to anticipate. These fertilizers are often less expensive than natural organic fertilizers and less bulky because they are more concentrated.

On the other hand, more work is usually required of gardeners using soluble synthetic fertilizers. Because their effects do not last as long, more applications are necessary. For example, if your lawn requires 4 to 6 pounds of actual nitrogen per 1,000 square feet per year for optimum maintenance, four to six separate applications are necessary during the growing season. With slower-acting natural organics, you might make only three to five.

Further, because of the high salt content of these fertilizers, there is the possibility of fertilizer burn. To avoid this, apply the fertilizer at recommended rates, spread it on a dry lawn, and water it in thoroughly after application.

Timed-release fertilizers Also referred to as controlled or slow-release fertilizers, these combine the characteristics of the natural organics and the soluble synthetics to some extent. Some of these products contain nitrogen as part of a complex compound that breaks down slowly in the soil. Others consist of pellets of quick-release nitrogen compound coated with a semipermeable resin or plastic-like material. Each time the pellets get wet, they release small amounts of nutrient through their coatings until they are fully depleted. Both types of products can last three to six months, depending on the brand and on how often they get wet. They usually contain a high percentage of nitrogen, so large quantities are not necessary. The possibility of fertilizer burn is greatly reduced, since the nitrogen does not become available to the plant all at once.

Several types of timed-release fertilizers are available. One of them, sulfur-coated urea (SCU) is made with coatings of differing thicknesses, which provide differing rates of release. Other timed-release fertilizers are synthetic organic materials that have low solubility in water. Two products in this category are urea formaldehyde (UF) and isobutylidene diurea (IBDU).

Many lawn growers prefer timed-release fertilizers because they can be applied at heavier rates than soluble synthetics, thus reducing the number of applications. However, they do not provide as quick a green-up, and they are more expensive. Many manufacturers mix soluble and coated fertilizer materials to ensure both rapid and long-term response.

Complete fertilizers Complete fertilizers are those that contain all three of the primary nutrients: nitrogen (in the form of nitrates or ammonium), phosphorus (in the form of phosphoric acid), and potassium (in the form of potash). The percentages (by weight) of these elements are prominently displayed on fertilizer labels as three numbers separated by dashes. The first number represents nitrogen, the second phosphorus, and the third potassium. For example, a product labeled 15-5-10 contains 15 percent nitrogen, 5 percent phosphorus, and 10 percent potassium as compared with the total weight of the contents. (The remaining 70 percent is inert material that helps distribute the nutrients evenly.) These percentages are called the analysis or the formula grade.

In complete fertilizers, a 3-1-2 ratio of nutrients has generally proved to be good for fertilizing home lawns. Although it is not critical that a fertilizer have exactly this ratio, something close to it is recommended. However, factors such as local climate, soil conditions, and the form of nitrogen in the fertilizer influence what is best in various localities.

For proper application, follow the directions on the label. Some complete fertilizers are manufactured for general use, while others are designed to be used on specific grasses.

Fertilizer, herbicide, and pesticide combinations In recent years, combinations of fertilizers and pesticides have become available and are widely used. Many combinations also contain herbicides for broadleaf weed or crabgrass control, while some products include insecticides, fungicides, or both.

These products have definite advantages. Considerable time, labor, and equipment are saved by accomplishing two or more jobs at once. Less material needs to be handled and less storage space is required. In addition, the cost of the combined material may be less than that of the ingredients when purchased separately.

The disadvantage of combining fertilizers and pesticides is the difficulty in applying the products at the proper time, since the best time to fertilize is not always the best time to control diseases, weeds, or insects. For best results, apply a combination product during the growth cycles of the diseases, weeds, or insects you wish to eradicate. A fertilizer combined with preventive chemicals is most useful if you fully understand its advantages and limitations, and if you adhere to the product directions carefully.

How Much Fertilizer to Apply

The amount of fertilizer needed by your lawn depends on many factors, including the desired lawn quality, the weather conditions, the length of the growing season, the soil texture, the level of sunlight or shade, the amount of foot traffic your lawn receives, how much it is watered, and whether grass clippings are removed from the lawn or left to decompose.

Fertilizer requirements also vary with the type of grass. In general, fast-growing grasses such as creeping bentgrass and hybrid bermudagrass are heavy feeders, whereas grasses that grow more slowly, such as centipedegrass and fine fescues, need significantly less fertilizer.

Although there are general rules regarding how much fertilizer to use, there are so many variables that determining exact amounts is more an art than a science. Only by observing the effects of fertilizer on your lawn can you learn how far you can depart from the norm.

Because fertilizers vary in formula and type, their application rates also differ. In order to determine how much fertilizer to use on your lawn, you first need to know how much *actual nitrogen* it requires. Actual nitrogen refers to the weight of the nitrogen in the fertilizer you are applying. For example, 24-4-8 fertilizer contains 24 percent nitrogen by weight; so a 100-pound bag of this fertilizer would contain 24 pounds of actual nitrogen, and a 50-pound bag would contain 12 pounds of actual nitrogen. The chart on page 71 lists the actual nitrogen requirements (per growing month) of common lawn grasses.

To calculate the amount of fertilizer to use on your lawn, divide the number of pounds of actual nitrogen the lawn needs by the percentage of nitrogen in the fertilizer you are using. For example, if you need to apply 1 pound of actual nitrogen per growing month, and you are using 24-4-8 fertilizer, divide 1 by .24. The result, 4.17, is the number of pounds of this fertilizer to apply each month per 1,000 square feet. If you fertilize less often than monthly, apply the amount of fertilizer the lawn would have received if you had given it monthly feedings. To avoid burning the lawn, be sure to water well after these heavy feedings.

Most fertilizer labels recommend application rates that supply approximately 1 pound of actual nitrogen per 1,000 square feet—the maximum rate needed by Kentucky bluegrass and several other popular grasses. Actually, however, many lawn grasses need far less. See the Actual Nitrogen Requirements chart on this page for the amount to use for your grass. Note that timed-release fertilizers are often applied at rates higher than 1 pound.

When to Fertilize

Many factors influence the rate at which lawns consume nutrients and therefore the frequency with which they need fertilizing. Although there are guidelines that can help you determine when to fertilize your lawn, it is an art best learned by practice. If the lawn grows too rapidly, and you have to mow it more than once a week, fertilize less. If it turns yellow, and you have been watering it regularly, this may signal either an iron deficiency (see page 106) or the need to fertilize more.

It is best to fertilize your lawn during periods when temperature and moisture conditions favor active growth of the lawn. Depending on the climate and the type of grass, this is usually from early spring to late fall. If you fertilize at the beginning of these periods rather than in the middle, your lawn will have full benefit of the additional nutrients during the entire time it is growing.

Actual Nitrogen Requirements

The chart below tells how much fertilizer different grasses require when maintained at a moderate to intensive level of care. To determine how much fertilizer to apply per 1,000 square feet each year, use these figures in the Fertilizer Worksheet on this page. Apply the lesser amount if your lawn is shaded or is growing too rapidly, and the higher amount if your lawn is in full sun or is growing too slowly. If your lawn contains a mixture of two or more grasses, use an average of their requirements.

Native grasses such as buffalograss need far less fertilizer than do domestic types, and are thus omitted from this list. They are best fertilized twice a year (in midspring and early fall) with a complete fertilizer such as 10-5-5 or 12-6-4.

Grass	Pounds of Actual Nitrogen Per Growing Month
Cool-Season Grasses	
Bentgrass, Creeping	½–1
Bluegrass, Kentucky	½–1
Bluegrass, Rough	¼–½
Fescue, Chewings	¼–½
Fescue, Dwarf	¼–½
Fescue, Hard	¼–½
Fescue, Red	¼–½
Fescue, Tall	¼–½
Ryegrass, Annual	¼–½
Ryegrass, Perennial	¼–½
Warm-Season Grasses	
Bahiagrass	¼–½
Bermudagrass, Common	½–1
Bermudagrass, Hybrid	¾–1
Centipedegrass	¹/₁₀–³/₁₀
St. Augustine Grass	½–1
Zoysiagrass	¼–½

Fertilizer Worksheet

To determine how much fertilizer to use per 1,000 square feet per growing month, complete the following calculations:

Pounds of actual nitrogen to apply (from the Actual Nitrogen Requirements chart)   [ ]

÷

Percentage of nitrogen in fertilizer (for example, 24% = .24)   [ ]

Pounds of fertilizer for each feeding (per 1,000 square feet)   [ ]

Left: A hose-end sprayer dispenses liquid fertilizer from a container attached to a nozzle.
Right: A handheld broadcast spreader, operated with a crank, applies granular fertilizer over a small area.

How to Apply Fertilizer

The most common methods of applying fertilizers are spraying, broadcast spreading, and drop spreading. Use a sprayer to apply liquid or water-soluble powdered fertilizer, and either a broadcast spreader or a drop spreader to apply a dry, granular fertilizer. You can purchase or rent both types of spreader from a nursery. Some nurseries will let regular customers use them without charge.

Always fill sprayers or spreaders over a sidewalk or driveway. If you happen to spill concentrated fertilizer on the lawn, hose it away or scrape or vacuum it up, then flood the area with water to avoid fertilizer burn.

Sprayers   The most common type of sprayer used to apply liquid fertilizer is a hose-end sprayer. This sprayer has a plastic or glass body suspended beneath a nozzle that attaches to the end of a hose. Water from the hose dilutes the liquid and propels it through the nozzle, spraying up to 15 gallons of fertilizer over a wide area.

To use a hose-end sprayer, simply measure concentrated liquid fertilizer into the sprayer container and fill it with water to the proper level. Spray the entire contents of the sprayer onto your lawn, providing equal coverage to all sections of it. Read the directions on both the liquid fertilizer and the sprayer carefully. Be accurate about the ratio of fertilizer to water,

and make sure all parts of the sprayer are operational and attached properly.

Broadcast spreaders   The easiest way to apply dry fertilizers is with a broadcast spreader. It is possible to spread these fertilizers by hand, but it is difficult to apply them evenly. Green streaks or burned areas can easily result from uneven application, so it is a good idea to use a spreader.

There are two types: handheld and push wheel. Each model throws the dry fertilizer over a wide area by means of a whirling wheel. The handheld broadcast spreader is operated by turning a side-arm crank, which turns a wheel that causes the fertilizer to fly outward. It is best for smaller lawns. The push wheel spreader flings fertilizer from the bottom of a large hopper as you wheel it across the lawn. Make sure to measure the throw width so that you can calculate how far to space your passes. You can determine the throw width easily by running the spreader over dark-colored pavement for a short distance. Usually, overlapping passes by one fourth of their width is sufficient for uniform coverage.

Because it requires fewer passes to completely cover the lawn, a push-type broadcast spreader is easier to use than a drop spreader, especially on large lawns. Streaking is also less likely with broadcast spreaders, because the swaths of fertilizer overlap and the edges of

Left: A push-wheel broadcast spreader flings fertilizer granules over a wide area.
Right: A drop spreader applies fertilizer more precisely than a broadcast spreader, but takes longer to cover the lawn.

the swaths are less distinct than those produced by drop spreaders.

The best technique for applying fertilizer with a broadcast spreader is to cover the ends of the lawn first, then go back and forth the long way. To avoid double applications, shut off the spreader as you approach the end strips. Keep the spreader closed while you are turning around, backing up, or stopped. For even and thorough coverage, walk at a normal speed and keep the spreader level.

Broadcast spreaders have adjustable settings. A chart that comes with the spreader tells you which setting to use for most brands of fertilizer. Although the settings are fairly accurate when the spreaders are new, they should be calibrated at least once a year.

One way to check the calibration is to draw a square 10 feet by 10 feet on a clean, smooth patio or driveway. Fill the spreader, then spread fertilizer over the square. Sweep up the fertilizer in the square and weigh it. Multiply the weight of the fertilizer by 10 to find how much will be spread over 1,000 square feet. If the amount is not what you want it to be, try another setting and repeat.

Another calibration method is to measure an area of lawn (such as 500 square feet) and weigh out the specified number of pounds of fertilizer to cover that area. Fill the hopper with fertilizer and adjust the dispenser to the setting specified on the fertilizer label. For example, if a hopperful of fertilizer weighs 3 pounds, and the label calls for 6 pounds per 1,000 square feet, then one hopperful should spread evenly over 500 square feet. If it does not, try another setting and repeat the test on another section of lawn.

Drop spreaders Drop spreaders are more precise than broadcast spreaders, but slower. They are most useful on small- and medium-sized lawns. When using a drop spreader, overlap the wheel tracks enough so that no strips are left underfertilized, but also be careful not to double-feed any sections. If this happens, your lawn will become green unevenly, or worse, it will develop fertilizer burn.

Like broadcast spreaders, drop spreaders have adjustable settings for use with different brands of fertilizer. It is a good idea to calibrate them yearly to ensure that they dispense fertilizer at the proper rate. To check the calibration, draw a square 10 feet by 10 feet on a clean, smooth patio or driveway. Fill the spreader, then spread fertilizer over the square. Sweep up the fertilizer in the square and weigh it. Multiply the weight of the fertilizer by 10 to find how much will be spread over 1,000 square feet. If the amount is not what you want it to be, try another setting and repeat.

Drop spreaders are also used to spread seed. Again, calibration is necessary to make sure you apply the appropriate quantities.

WINTER AND THE LAWN

All lawns undergo some change and reduction of growth during the winter months, whether they are growing in a warm climate or a cold one. The way a lawn responds to winter depends on several factors: the variety of the grass, the winter temperatures, the amount of snowfall, and the type of care the lawn has received, particularly in the months just preceding winter.

Wherever you live, there are things you can do to help your lawn survive winter and recover vigorously in spring.

Cool-Season Grasses

In the northern regions where cool-season grasses thrive, lawns may be frozen or snow covered for much of the winter. In many places, people cannot even see their lawns let alone care for them. While your lawn is under snow, there is little you can or need to do for it. If it was well cared for before winter arrived, your lawn should have no trouble surviving until spring.

That said, there are still a number of steps you can take to keep cool-season grasses in better condition during the coldest months. Here are a few suggestions.

• A month before colder temperatures begin, fertilize the lawn with a complete fertilizer (one that contains nitrogen, phosphorus, and potassium), such as 15-5-10. Depending on your location, this may be in September, October, or November. The complete fertilizer helps prepare

New shoots appear in a cool-season lawn that has gone dormant during freezing weather. A well-maintained lawn will easily survive winter.

the roots and leaves to withstand cooler weather.

• If your area has experienced a summer drought, it is a good idea to aerate your lawn in the fall so that any winter precipitation can more easily penetrate the grass and soil.

• Snow can act as an insulation for lawns and should be allowed to remain on the grass if normal winter temperatures in the area fall below 32° F. Since the snow itself is 32° F, it can help keep the grass below it from getting very much colder, even if the soil beneath the grass freezes to a lower temperature. You may want to put up snow fences to help keep the snow from blowing away.

• In late winter, when melting snow exposes grass to cold and wind, consider watering the lawn to keep it from drying out.

• While the lawn is frozen or snow covered, keep traffic over it to a minimum. Frequent walking across a frozen lawn can wear it out.

• When winter is over and temperatures begin to rise, rake your lawn vigorously to rid it of debris and to help stimulate new growth in the existing grass. To fill in bare spots, lightly seed the lawn and cover the seeded areas with a thin layer of top dressing.

Warm-Season Grasses

The warm-season grasses typically grown in southern regions usually go dormant in winter, turning yellow or brown and remaining so until temperatures warm up in spring. This dormancy can occur in even the warmest areas, although it does not occur there every year—usually because temperatures are not cold enough to cause such a distinct color change.

Because southerly regions are rarely snow covered, dormant lawns can be an eyesore, particularly if nearby plantings are still lush and green. The best way to keep a warm-season lawn green over the winter is to overseed it with a cool-season grass. This hides the dormant warm-season grass and provides a fresh, green temporary lawn. If you do not want to go to the effort of overseeding, an alternative is to spray your lawn with a colorant, a special dye available from agricultural chemical companies.

Overseeding Overseeding a warm-season grass with a cool-season variety enables you to have a green lawn throughout the year. Annual ryegrass is the most popular grass for overseeding because it grows and greens up quickly, then conveniently dies out in summer when the main grass revives. Other grasses can also be used; several seed companies produce mixes and blends specifically for winter overseeding.

Because cool-season grasses germinate best when temperatures are falling, you should start overseeding when temperatures begin to drop, typically in October or November. If you start too early, the warm-season grass will still be active and will crowd out the cool-season grass. If you start too late, cold weather may inhibit seed germination.

Normally, you can simply spread the seeds over the existing lawn and water them in. If the lawn has heavy thatch, however, you need to take extra steps to ensure close contact between the seeds and the soil. Mow close to the soil line with a heavy reel or rotary mower, rake up the clippings, then mow and rake again. Or use a vertical mower (available from equipment rental companies) to slice shallow grooves into the lawn. If possible, dethatch and aerate the lawn as well (see pages 75 to 77).

You should then sow two to three times as much seed as you would for a new lawn (use the larger amounts where temperatures are colder), and finish by covering the seeded area with ½ inch of topsoil or top dressing. Water frequently until the new grass is firmly rooted. Once the cool-season grass is established, mow at a height of about 2 inches.

The following spring, encourage the regrowth of the warm-season grass by closely mowing the cool-season cover. Then fertilize at the recommended rate for the type of warm-season grass you have.

Overseeding also has other uses. In summer, a cool-season grass can be overseeded with a more wear-tolerant cool-season grass to improve its endurance of foot traffic. A shady area can be overseeded with a more shade-tolerant grass to help it survive under trees.

Lawn colorants   Special green dyes or latex paints, made especially for coloring dormant warm-season lawns, are an alternative to winter overseeding. These can also be used in summer on cool-season lawns browned by heat or drought. High-quality colorants are fadeproof, nontoxic, and long lasting. They wear off eventually, but usually not before warm temperatures revive the dormant grass. A nursery or agricultural extension service can tell you where to buy these products.

In winter, make the first application of colorant when the grass starts to lose its color. In summer, apply it when the grass begins turning yellowish or brownish. Before applying the colorant, mow and edge the lawn carefully and remove all debris. Tape off the edges of sidewalks and driveways, then apply the colorant evenly with a compression sprayer and let it dry for several hours. See the product label for more complete instructions.

AERATING AND DETHATCHING

Lawns cannot live without air, water, and nutrients. When air has been squeezed out of the soil by heavy trampling, roots cannot grow as efficiently. When a thick layer of thatch builds up above the soil line, water and fertilizer may run off instead of penetrating the soil. The lawn may therefore suffer slow starvation even in the midst of plenty.

Aerating and dethatching can help rejuvenate a lawn by restoring passageways to the soil. Although these tasks are performed infrequently, they are just as important to a lawn's long-term survival as are routine fertilizing and mowing. You can perform both of them yourself with hand tools, but your job will be easier if you rent specialized power equipment, especially if your lawn is large.

Aerating

Many lawns, particularly those that receive heavy use, have compacted soil that restricts the movement of air and water to the roots. A footpath worn into a lawn is a visible example of compaction.

To correct compacted soil, it is necessary to aerate your lawn from time to time. Poor drainage, failure to turn green after fertilizing, and the presence of many worn areas may all signal the need to aerate. Intensively maintained lawns should be aerated about once a year; those receiving moderate maintenance need aerating every two years or so. Lawns with severe thatch problems or heavily compacted soils may require two aerations per year, even if other maintenance activities are minimal.

Aeration consists of perforating the soil (and any thatch above it) with small holes that

Top left: A power-driven core aerator has hollow spikes that pull up plugs of turf to create openings in the soil.
Top right: A foot-press aerator accomplishes the same task, only more slowly.
Bottom: With a two-inch layer of dead grass stems, this lawn is overdue for dethatching.

allow water, air, and fertilizer to get closer to the roots. This enables the roots to grow more deeply, producing a more vigorous lawn.

One of the most useful functions of aeration is to penetrate the layer of thatch that forms a water barrier over the soil. Breaking through thatch with an aeration device is far easier and less drastic than dethatching, and is almost as effective. In fact, aeration is better than dethatching in some ways because it causes less stress to the grass and leaves less debris behind.

To aerate a lawn, use one of several specialized tools to punch holes into the soil. Available for sale or rent, these tools range from motorized aerating machines to foot-press aerators that you push into the soil like a shovel.

The better aerating tools remove thin cigar-shaped plugs of earth and deposit them on the surface of the lawn. These plugs are left to dry for a day, then broken up by energetic raking or by mowing with a side-chute lawn mower. This creates a thin, beneficial top dressing. Some other, less effective aerating tools punch

narrow holes into the soil without removing plugs. Whichever tool you use, make sure that soil is moist during aeration—neither too wet nor too dry—so that the aerating device can penetrate it easily.

Aeration is not usually a difficult job, but you may wish to hire a professional if you find the work too strenuous.

Dethatching

Thatch is a layer of slowly decomposing grass stems, dead roots, and debris that accumulates above the soil and below grass blades. The name thatch is well deserved. Like the thatched roof on a tropical hut, it stops water and fertilizer from reaching the soil. A lawn with a buildup of thatch feels spongy when you walk on it.

Thatch is a problem only when it becomes too thick. A thin layer of thatch ¼ to ½ inch thick may actually be beneficial to the lawn. It buffers soil temperatures and adds to the resilience of the lawn, thereby reducing the compaction of soil that can result from heavy use.

When thick, however, thatch is hydrophobic, or water repellent. Conscientious gardeners may think they are watering enough, when in fact the water never reaches the soil. Grass roots that grow in the thatch layer instead of in the soil are less drought resistant, since the moisture in the thatch evaporates faster than the moisture that penetrates the soil.

Although all lawn grasses have the potential for developing thatch, it accumulates the fastest in lawns composed of creeping grasses. Notorious thatch builders include warm-season grasses such as bermudagrass, St. Augustine grass, and zoysiagrass, and cool-season grasses such as bentgrass and Kentucky bluegrass. Thatch also accumulates faster in extremely acid soils, where the microorganisms that decompose thatch are less active.

Insects and diseases find thatch a particularly suitable place to inhabit. Since water does not penetrate it readily, neither do pest and disease control products. It may take two to three weeks to control soil insects like grubs under a lawn with thatch—as opposed to half that long in a thatch-free lawn.

Finally, because the thickness and density of thatch varies, lawn mowers are more likely to cut unevenly, causing scalping (page 106).

What to do about thatch Dethatching is typically performed every other year, although the actual frequency depends on the type of grass. Examining your lawn is the best way to tell whether it needs dethatching. Take note if fertilizers and insecticides do not seem to be working, and probe with your fingers to determine how thick the thatch is.

The best time to dethatch is just before a lawn has its most vigorous growth of the season. Dethatch warm-season grasses with the beginning of warm weather in late spring. Prime time for dethatching cool-season grasses is late spring or early fall.

Aeration is the most useful treatment for moderate thatch. For heavier thatch, several remedies are available. Soil penetrants, or wetting agents, counteract the hydrophobic character of thatch, but only briefly. Bacterial agents that help break down thatch have proved somewhat effective, though again not long lasting. Thatching rakes with knifelike blades instead of teeth are useful for small lawns. Special attachments for rotary mowers, such as thatching rakes, may be helpful.

The most effective way to dethatch a home lawn is with a vertical mower. Resembling a heavy-duty power mower, a vertical mower has a series of revolving vertical knives that cut and pull through the thatch and bring it to the surface of the lawn. You then sweep, rake, or vacuum this material away. Vertical mowers may be rented from local equipment rental companies.

To dethatch effectively, adjust the depth and spacing of the vertical mower blades for your type of grass. Generally, the blades should completely penetrate the top half of the thatch layer. Move the vertical mower across the lawn in parallel rows; then mow again in a crosswise direction. For thatch thicker than 1 inch, mow a third time at a 45-degree angle with the previous cuts.

If you have eliminated a great deal of thatch from your lawn, you can help the lawn recover by applying a complete fertilizer and watering it in.

Unless you are removing dead grass prior to renovating (see page 109), dethatching a lawn severely with a vertical mower is probably unwise. If the lawn and its roots are well established, severe dethatching can weaken the turf and disturb the soil, allowing difficult grassy weeds such as coarse fescue to gain a foothold. It is thus best to set the blades of the vertical mower so that they disturb the soil surface as little as possible. It is better to do a mild dethatching frequently than to do a severe tearing or stripping that approaches the disruptiveness of rotary tilling.

If you suspect that your thatch buildup was promoted by extremely acid soil, test the pH and add lime if necessary. The beneficial microorganisms that decompose thatch are most active at a slightly acid to neutral pH of 6.0 to 7.0.

Left: Useful for small lawns, a thatching rake has blades that slice through turf to bring thatch to the surface.
Right: A power-driven vertical mower has rotating vertical blades that rapidly cut out thatch. It performs the same function as a thatching rake.

Problem-Solving Guide

Even the best-maintained lawns may have problems from time to time. This chapter will help you identify and solve them.

Diagnosing lawn problems is often difficult, especially if considerable time has elapsed between the cause of the damage and the diagnosis. A problem that is attributed to an insect or a disease may have actually been caused by an environmental condition, such as soil compaction or flooding. Or it may have arisen from improper cultural practices, such as using too much fertilizer or herbicide. These stresses, in turn, could have weakened the grass and paved the way for insects or diseases—thereby making the problem even harder to solve.

If your lawn does not look very good, consult the pictures and descriptions in this chapter. Your local nursery or agricultural extension service may be able to help you with the diagnosis. If your lawn has been seriously damaged, you may want to consider replacing it with a more resistant grass. You will find instructions for this undertaking on pages 108 and 109.

Dandelions look cheerful in a lawn, but are best eliminated before their feathery seeds can spread them near and far.

Weeds spread prolifically. If left unchecked, they will eventually crowd out lawn grasses.

WEEDS

Weeds are simply plants that grow where they are not wanted. Although most lawn weeds are broadleaf plants, even grasses can be weeds. For example, tall fescue is a valuable grass for highly trafficked lawns. But when it appears as a clump amid bermudagrass or Kentucky bluegrass, it is considered a weed.

Weed seeds permeate most soils by the millions. Some average weed plants can give rise to more than twenty thousand seeds. One common lawn weed, purslane, can produce more than two million seeds *per plant* in a single season.

Weed seeds are dispersed in many ways: by wind, animals, humans, lawn equipment, and soil amendments. Once in the soil, they wait, dormant, until brought to the surface or until the lawn dies, giving them more light and moisture to start growing. Some seeds remain alive in the soil for many years, which is why it is good to kill all existing weeds before putting in a new lawn. Although this will not guarantee

permanent freedom from weeds, it does cut down on them substantially while the lawn is becoming established.

Weeds gain a foothold more easily in lawns that are poorly maintained. Overwatering or underwatering, fertilizing too little or too much, and mowing too low can all tip the balance in favor of weeds. So can excessive wear, disease or insect damage, soil compaction, poor drainage, too much shade, or any condition that exposes the soil to extra light.

If your lawn has many weeds, the first step is to correct any underlying lawn care problems. Creating a healthy climate for your lawn automatically creates an unhealthy one for weeds.

Categories of Weeds

Lawn weeds are classified according to their longevity and the type of leaves they have. Because certain weed killers are more effective against one type of plant than another, it is important to know what kinds of weeds you are up against.

All weed plants are either annuals, biennials, or perennials. Annuals grow, set seed, and die within a year. There are summer annuals and winter annuals. Summer annuals germinate in spring, grow to maturity during summer, and die by fall or winter. Crabgrass, knotweed, and purslane are summer annuals. Winter annuals germinate in fall or early winter and overwinter in a vegetative state (without flowering). In spring they flower, produce a crop of seeds, and die. Examples of winter annuals are annual bluegrass, burclover, and chickweed. In warmer climates, some annuals such as crabgrass can live into a second year.

Biennials live for two years. The first year's growth is vegetative, usually as a low cluster of leaves. During the second year a flower stalk arises and produces seeds, and the plant dies. Mallow is an example of a biennial weed.

Perennials live and produce seeds year after year. Many perennial plants, such as bermudagrass, also reproduce by vegetative means. When underground rhizomes or aboveground stolons break off from the mother plant, each new section develops roots and leaves and becomes a separate plant.

Lawn weeds are further classified as either broadleaf or narrowleaf. (There are annuals, biennials, and perennials in both categories.) Broadleaf plants, also known as dicots, emerge from the soil with two small leaves; narrowleaf plants, or monocots, start out with a single leaf. Dandelion, mallow, and plantain are typical broadleaf weeds. Bermudagrass, annual bluegrass, and crabgrass are some common narrowleaf weeds.

Controlling Existing Weeds

Pulling lawn weeds by hand can be a tiresome, overwhelming, and usually futile job. The most effective way to remove existing weeds is to apply a postemergent herbicide, a chemical that kills weeds after they have emerged from the soil.

In general, annuals are the easiest and perennials the hardest weeds to destroy with a chemical herbicide. Since both are most vulnerable at the seedling stage, you have a better chance of killing them if you apply herbicides soon after the weeds germinate.

Postemergent herbicides are categorized as either contact or systemic. Contact herbicides kill aboveground plant parts that are covered by the spray. Systemic herbicides enter the weeds through their roots or leaves and move through the plants internally. Within a week or two, the systemic herbicide kills all parts of the plant.

Perennial weeds such as bermudagrass and nutsedge can send out new growth from below the soil surface. Since most contact herbicides destroy only the upper parts of these plants, the roots and underground buds remain undamaged. That is why it is essential to use a systemic herbicide, which is absorbed by even deep-growing roots.

Contact and systemic herbicides are further divided into selective and nonselective types. Selective herbicides kill one kind of plant but not another. If applied properly, they can control a number of broadleaf weeds without harming mature grass. This type is often used in weed-and-feed-type products that fertilize the lawn and kill weeds at the same time.

Nonselective herbicides, also known as vegetation killers, control both broadleaf and narrowleaf plants. These products are usually sprayed on the entire lawn to kill it prior to removal or replanting (see page 109). Some, such as glyphosate, can also be used as a spot treatment for wild grasses or other weeds growing in an existing lawn.

Postemergent herbicides can be applied in granular form, either by hand or with a handheld broadcaster or a push-type drop or broadcast spreader. They can also be applied in liquid form with a tank-type or hose-end sprayer.

It is absolutely critical to follow instructions exactly when using herbicides on a lawn. Less-than-desirable results can occur if proper application procedures are not followed.

Keeping Weed Seeds from Germinating

One of the best ways to help prevent weeds from invading an existing lawn is to use a preemergent herbicide so that they never get a chance to grow. These herbicides form a chemical barrier near the soil surface and destroy susceptible seeds or seedlings before weeds emerge. Preemergent herbicide is used primarily to control annual grasses and broadleaf weeds before they appear in a permanent lawn. Mature, established grasses are not killed by preemergent herbicides because their roots are beneath the chemical barrier. However, never apply a preemergent herbicide to a newly seeded lawn because the chemical could kill it. Read the product label to determine which grasses can tolerate it.

The chemical barrier formed at the soil surface by preemergent herbicides usually lasts six to twelve weeks, depending on the chemical used. Eventually, microorganisms break down the herbicide.

Proper timing of an application is very important. Preemergent herbicides should be applied to an established lawn one to two weeks before weed-seed germination, usually just as the soil begins to warm up in early spring, and again in early fall. They have little effect if applied after the weeds have emerged. However, they should not be applied too long before the seeds of annual grasses start to germinate, because germination continues for a number of weeks. If the chemical is put down too early, it may lose its effectiveness before the peak germinating period ends.

Both liquid and granular formulations are equally effective. In southern states and warm regions of the West, two applications per growing season are usually necessary. Some preemergent herbicides can damage ornamental plants and even some desirable lawn plants, such as bentgrass and dichondra. Be sure to heed all cautions on the label and follow the instructions exactly.

COMMON LAWN WEEDS

Pictured in the following pages are common weeds that crop up in lawns in the United States and Canada. You will probably recognize at least a few of these in your own lawn. Some are broadleaf plants; others are narrowleaf grasses. Annuals, biennials, and perennials are represented.

Identifying the weeds in your lawn is the first step in any control program. If you cannot identify a weed from these photographs, take a sample to your local nursery or county agricultural service. They should be able to name the weed and tell you how to control it. Many state agricultural extension services offer useful publications on weed control.

The existence of a particular weed in your lawn can be a clue to an underlying problem. For example, crabgrass and dallisgrass grow in soggy places, indicating possible poor drainage. Curly dock tends to invade lawns overstressed by heat and drought. Correcting the problem may be enough to discourage the weeds.

Note that the herbicides named here are active ingredients that may be found in more than one product. Your local garden center can guide you to products containing the ingredients you need. Because the list of approved herbicides changes periodically, check with your garden center or county extension service for the latest information.

Broadleaf Weeds

Burclover
Medicago hispida
This prostrate, spreading annual weed hugs the ground and becomes especially unsightly in closely mowed lawns. Growing most rapidly during spring and fall, its creeping stems may vary in length from a few inches to several feet. The yellow-orange flowers give way to barbed seedpods that attach themselves to almost anything that moves.

No preemergent controls are available, but a product containing dicamba or MCPP can be used in spring or fall for postemergent control. Hand weeding is often done in small lawns.

Curly Dock
Rumex crispus
Growing from a large, brownish taproot, curly dock is a perennial weed that grows most actively when grass is suffering from the stress of hot, dry weather. Its leaves are bright, shiny green in spring and edged with reddish purple in summer and fall. If not removed, curly dock sends up a tall, narrow spike of greenish flowers from the center of the plant.

Pull out curly dock by hand or with a small spade. For heavy infestations, apply dicamba or 2,4-D in midspring or midfall for postemergent control. Because curly dock has a tenacious root system, preemergent controls (which act only on seeds) will not combat this weed effectively.

Guidelines for Weed Control

Here are some guidelines to observe when applying herbicides to your lawn.
• Herbicides generally work best on young, succulent weeds. The weeds should be actively growing at the time of application to ensure that they absorb the material efficiently.
• For maximum effectiveness, use herbicides when the soil is moist and warm. These conditions favor the most rapid growth of weeds, and hence the most efficient uptake of herbicides. If the soil is dry before treatment, water the lawn two days before applying the herbicide. Avoid using herbicides during hot weather (over 80° F), when damage to desirable grasses is more likely.
• Do not mow the lawn right before applying an herbicide. If you do, you will be cutting off vulnerable leaf tissue on the weeds, wasting the effects of the herbicide.
• When applying postemergent herbicides, it is better to spot-treat weeds rather than to apply herbicides over the entire lawn. These herbicides do no good where weeds are not growing, and they can harm desirable grasses.
• Avoid drift. If it is windy, do not spray. If you are using granular material, keep the spreader close to the lawn surface so that the herbicide does not stray onto nearby plants.
• For proper effectiveness and safety, use herbicides only at the concentration indicated on the label. Use neither more nor less.
• If you are using a granular material, the weed leaves should be moist before application. This will help the herbicide stick better. For the same reason, keep traffic off the treated area for at least eight hours.
• Unless the product is labeled otherwise, apply the herbicide at least eight hours and preferably at least 24 hours before anticipated rain or lawn watering.
• Do not mow for two days after the application. Mowing immediately will remove the herbicide before it can start to work.
• Wait at least two weeks before retreatment. Be patient—it may take up to four weeks for the weeds to die.
• Grass seedlings are very sensitive to herbicides. It is best to delay applications until a newly planted area has been mowed at least three times.
• Do not apply any herbicides to newly installed sod until it is firmly rooted.
• Do not use grass clippings on gardens or around shrubs if herbicides have been applied. Herbicide residue may still be present on the clippings and could harm the ornamental plants.

Burclover

Curly dock

Dandelion
Taraxacum officinale

Dandelion is a common perennial that appears mostly in spring and fall. It has a long, fleshy taproot. Its yellow blossoms make it probably the most easily recognized of all lawn weeds. At maturity, the flower becomes a fluffy white ball of feathery seeds that can be carried many miles by the wind. A single plant can be a continual source of infestation as more flowers mature. To discourage seeds from sprouting, promote heavier grass growth by conscientious fertilizing, and mow at the high end of the range for your grass.

One reason dandelions are difficult to control is that new shoots quickly develop from even a small piece of remaining root when the weed is hand pulled or cut off at the crown. To prevent this from happening, pull out young plants before the taproot has a chance to grow deeply. Sprays containing MCPP or 2,4-D are also effective on growing plants. Apply them in early spring and early fall when growth is active and temperatures are between 60° and 80° F. Control is least effective when dandelions are in full bloom.

English Daisy
Bellis perennis

Originally grown as an ornamental, English daisy has long since escaped the flower garden and become a well-established lawn weed on the West Coast. The leaves of this perennial vary from nearly smooth to hairy, forming an extremely dense cluster. The daisylike flowers on 2-inch stalks have bright yellow centers with white to pinkish outer rays.

Dandelion

English daisy

Henbit

Knotweed

Mouse-ear chickweed

Oxalis

English daisy can form extensive patches in a very short time. It grows most rapidly in the cool weather of spring and fall, and in all seasons on the West Coast if protected from drought and high heat.

There are no preemergent controls for English daisy, and it is difficult to eradicate once established. Dicamba, MCPP, or 2,4-D work fairly well against growing plants. Apply as the label directs to control any regrowth or new seedlings.

Henbit
Lamium amplexicaule

This annual makes its first appearance in late winter or early spring. Its stems lie close to the ground, then curve and grow upright, often rooting at lower nodes. A member of the mint family, henbit has the typical square-shaped main stem of these plants. Flowers are trumpet shaped and pale purple.

This plant can become a problem in early spring. New herbicides are being developed for preemergent control but are not yet available to the home gardener. For postemergent control, use dicamba, MCPP, or 2,4-D in fall or spring. Two applications may be required.

Knotweed
Polygonum aviculare

Knotweed prefers the hard, beaten paths across turf and the compact soil next to driveways. It is an annual plant that germinates with the first warm temperatures of spring. Often the homeowner mistakes these first tiny shoots as a welcome cover of new grass. However, they soon branch out to form a wiry, tough, prostrate mat. Tiny white flowers appear at the junction of leaf and stem.

Knotweed not only prevents the growth of desirable grass, but also produces vast numbers of seeds for the following year. Use benefin for preemergent control. For postemergent treatment use products containing dicamba, MCPP, or 2,4-D from mid to late spring. Spot applications of glyphosate can be used to kill individual plants.

Mouse-Ear Chickweed
Cerastium vulgatum

Many lawn weeds can be held in check by frequent mowings, but mouse-ear chickweed is not one of these. This perennial hugs the ground, and mowing only stimulates a more vigorous habit of prostrate growth. The softly hairy leaves appear opposite each other on stems in an arrangement suggestive of the plant's name. The hairy stems creep along the ground and take root wherever leaf nodes touch the soil. Flowers are small and white with five slightly notched petals. Chickweed seeds are sometimes a contaminant in cheap grass seed mixtures.

Mouse-ear chickweed grows very well in bright sunshine, especially in the cool weather of spring or fall.

For preemergent control, use atrazine in centipedegrass, St. Augustine grass, and zoysiagrass lawns, or DCPA in cool-season lawns. Once the weed is established, postemergent products containing dicamba or MCPP can be applied in fall or early spring when temperatures are above 60° F.

Oxalis
Oxalis corniculata, Oxalis stricta
This is an upright perennial or annual that sends out roots from its lower nodes. Its trios of leaflets closely resemble those of clover. Flowers are small, with five bright yellow petals. As flowers mature, cucumber-shaped seed pods take their place. When pods are completely dry, the slightest touch will send seeds scattering for several feet in all directions. Oxalis grows most vigorously in spring and late summer to fall.

Keeping the lawn well fertilized and vigorously growing will help keep oxalis in check. Oryzalin and pendimethalin are effective preemergent controls.

Postemergent products containing dicamba, MCPP, 2,4-D, or 2,4-DP may be used. Apply these in spring or fall on a day when the wind is still and air temperatures are between 60° and 80° F. Several treatments may be required for good control.

Perennial Slender Speedwell
Veronica filiformis
Growing most vigorously in spring and fall, this annual or perennial weed forms dense patches that become established below the height of a lawn mower, making it difficult to kill. These patches gradually suffocate the lawn. Flowers are light blue; several similar species have bright blue to purple flowers. Distinctive heart-shaped seed capsules containing numerous seeds are arranged along the stem below the tiny flowers.

For best control, spray in fall with postemergent herbicides containing 2,4-D; or at flowering time in spring with DCPA. Two applications of either product may be necessary.

Plantain
Plantago species
These perennials are found in practically all soils. The rosette of prominently veined leaves lies flat on the ground and has a tendency to suffocate desirable grasses. The flower stalk is long and slender and curls slightly at the top. Seeds are compressed like a coating along the wiry stalks.

Atrazine can be used as a preemergent control for plantain in centipedegrass, St. Augustine grass, and zoysiagrass. For postemergent control (in warm-season grasses) and as a spot treatment (in cool-season grasses), MCPP or 2,4-D are effective when applied in spring or fall before the flower spikes form. Clumps can be cut out if care is taken to get well under the root crown, so that no roots remain to grow anew. Conscientious lawn care will help develop a lawn that resists further invasion.

Perennial slender speedwell

Plantain

Purslane

Spotted spurge

White clover

Purslane
Portulaca oleracea
In new seedings or thin lawns, purslane can become one of the most troublesome summer annual weeds. It can thrive in extremely hot, dry weather. The sprawling stems are thick and fleshy with rubbery leaves. Tiny yellow five-petaled flowers seldom open unless the sun is shining brightly. Cup-shaped seedpods produce many small black seeds that may lie dormant in the soil for years.

For preemergent control, apply DCPA from early to midspring. For postemergent control, use dicamba, 2,4-D, or triclopyr from midsummer to late summer as a spot treatment in nonlawn areas. Atrazine is effective in centipedegrass, St. Augustine grass, and zoysiagrass lawns as a pre- or postemergent weed killer.

Spotted Spurge
Euphorbia maculata
From late spring through early fall, the spreading branches of this annual choke and often suffocate desirable grasses. Flowers are pinkish white and inconspicuous. When broken, stems and branches exude a milky substance.

For preemergent control in grass lawns, use an herbicide containing DCPA or pendimethalin. Apply in early spring before the weeds germinate, then again in midsummer. Atrazine, another preemergent control, is effective in centipedegrass, St. Augustine grass, and zoysiagrass lawns. For postemergent control, use products containing dicamba, MCPP, or 2,4-D while the spurge is still young and before cool-season lawn grasses are under stress from drought or high temperatures. Reapply the product a week later if spurge continues to grow. Repeat throughout the summer as more seeds germinate.

White Clover
Trifolium repens
This familiar low-growing perennial is characterized by three-leaflet leaves and numerous white flowers resembling pom-poms. It spreads by creeping stems that root where nodes touch the soil. Often included in grass mixtures in the past, it is still added to some of the cheaper mixtures. Although it looks pleasant initially, clover soon suffocates desirable lawn grasses, then fades in hot weather and leaves large dead patches behind.

Atrazine will give preemergent control of clover in centipedegrass, St. Augustine grass, and zoysiagrass lawns. Postemergent control can be accomplished by applying dicamba, 2,4-D, or MCPP in spring or fall. It is best to choose a warm and windless day for treatment.

Supplying enough nitrogen in spring and fall will help the grass grow vigorously and crowd out clover. Limiting the amount of phosphorus (by using a nitrogen-only fertilizer) may also help.

Narrowleaf Weeds

Annual Bluegrass
Poa annual

This annual plant forms a mat when allowed to mature without cutting. Small wheatlike seed blossoms grow on top of the grass, giving it a whitish appearance. The seeds continue to form even under extremely close mowing. This weed is usually found in cool, frequently watered areas, shaded areas, and areas of compacted soil. It thrives in the cool weather of spring and fall, and tends to die out in summer. When it does, it leaves bare spots that may be mistaken for diseased areas. It is considered a winter annual in the South, where it is often used for winter overseeding.

For preemergent control use atrazine, benefin, bensulide, or DCPA. In early August through early October, it may be necessary to make several applications. For postemergent control, spot-treat with glyphosate or fluazifop-butyl and reseed the affected area.

Bermudagrass, Devilgrass
Cynodon dactylon

Bermudagrass is a perennial that grows fast when temperatures are high. Where it is well adapted to the climate, it can either be your lawn or your most troublesome weed if you have a different type of grass.

Spreading by rhizomes and stolons, bermudagrass can easily invade surrounding plant beds or a lawn consisting of a different, more desirable grass. The stolons are many-jointed, with roots forming at the nodes. Only heavy shade discourages it. Brown and dead looking in winter, it comes back to life in spring with renewed vigor.

No preemergent controls are available. It is important to remove the entire underground portion of the stem, or it will grow new shoots. Postemergent control can include repeated spot treatments of glyphosate in fall, or fluazifop-butyl in early spring. The treated areas will need to be reseeded after the bermudagrass has died.

Crabgrass
Digitaria species

This vigorous summer annual grows rapidly from early spring until seed heads form in late summer to early fall. It grows especially well in

Annual bluegrass

Bermudagrass, Devilgrass

Crabgrass

lawns that are watered lightly, underfertilized, poorly drained, and growing thinly. Crabgrass spreads by seed, and to a lesser extent by rooting from lower swollen nodes of stems. Some kinds have hairy leaves.

Products containing benefin, bensulide, DCPA, oxadiazon, or pendimethalin can be used for preemergent control in spring before seedlings appear. However, do not use these products on lawns containing bentgrass, centipedegrass,

Dallisgrass

Quackgrass

Tall fescue

Quackgrass

Agropyron repens

One of the most unwelcome perennial narrowleaf weeds, quackgrass spreads rapidly by starting new plants from strong, vigorous rhizomes. Narrow flower spikes that rise from the plant resemble slender heads of rye or wheat. If quackgrass is not mowed, it can grow 3 feet high.

Because quackgrass rhizomes are so vigorous, digging out these plants by hand is rarely successful. No preemergent control is available, but spot treatment with fluazifop-butyl or glyphosate can eliminate growing plants. Frequent close mowing reduces the weed's nutrient reserves and eventually kills it.

Tall Fescue

Festuca arundinacea

Tall fescue is a perennial that makes a good lawn where it is desired and well adapted, but a weed when it grows in a finer-textured lawn. Its leaf blades are wide and coarse, radiating from a central clump. The flower stalks lie flat during mowing, which can result in a ragged-looking lawn.

Growing especially vigorously in spring and fall, tall fescue can be either pulled out (by cutting under the root crown) or spot treated with postemergent herbicides containing glyphosate or fluazifop-butyl. If the clump was large, reseed the area or patch it with sod. There are no preemergent controls for tall fescue.

or St. Augustine grass, which may be damaged by them. Use organic arsenicals such as CAMA or MSMA for postemergent control when weeds are small and easier to combat. If needed, repeat the postemergent treatment after 10 to 14 days.

Dallisgrass

Paspalum dilatatum

A perennial, dallisgrass is a summer weed that grows throughout the year in mild climates. It has a bunch-type growth that is leafy at the base. Its rhizomes are closely jointed, appearing almost scaly. Seed heads are sparsely branched on long stems.

Dallisgrass thrives in low, wet areas, and draining or building up the lawn may be necessary to help control it. There are no preemergent controls on the market, but hand weeding can be effective. Reseeding will be necessary if many clumps of dallisgrass are removed from the lawn.

Postemergent controls include CAMA and MSMA, applied as a spot spray every 14 days or as the label directs. Do not use them on centipedegrass or St. Augustine grass.

Moss

Mushrooms

Other Weed Plants

Moss and Algae

These weed plants usually appear in lawns as a result of poor drainage or air circulation, too much shade, or too little fertilizer. Moss is a green, velvety, low-growing collection of tiny plants that covers bare soil in shaded areas. Algae appear as green to black, slimy scum that cover both bare soil and green lawn areas.

If you cannot control moss by raking, use 4 to 6 ounces of ferrous sulfate or 10 ounces of ferrous ammonium sulfate per 1,000 square feet. Algae are controlled with 2 to 3 ounces per 1,000 square feet of copper sulfate, or 2 to 3 pounds per 1,000 square feet of hydrated lime.

These treatments for moss and algae are only temporary. For a permanent solution, improve the general environment.

Mushrooms

After prolonged periods of wet weather, you may notice mushrooms coming up in the lawn. This often indicates the underground presence of decaying organic matter, such as construction debris or old tree roots and stumps. Most mushrooms cause no damage to the lawn. If they grow in circles of dark green grass, called fairy rings, the rings may injure the grass by making it impervious to water; see page 100 for advice.

There is no effective chemical control for mushrooms. If you feel that they are unsightly, remove them with a rake or lawn mower.

INSECTS AND OTHER PESTS

Hundreds of kinds of insects and other creatures live in a typical lawn. Some are so tiny they are hardly visible; others are quite large. Most do little damage to the lawn, and you are usually not even aware of their presence. Other insects such as fleas and ticks are troublesome to people and pets but do not damage the grass. Only a few lawn pests, such as billbugs, chinch bugs, grubs, and sod webworms, can destroy a lawn within a short time.

Serious damage by insects and other small pests can be prevented by inspecting your lawn regularly and by acting promptly against unwelcome intruders. Look for areas that are discolored, stunted, or distorted in their growth. By detecting symptoms early, you may be able to prevent the rapid buildup of pest populations. Some pests feed only at night, so unless you make an effort to look for their symptoms, they may go undetected. Other pests are present or destructive only at certain times of year.

Good control depends on correct identification of the pest and some knowledge of its behavior, its biology, and the conditions that favor it. Some pests thrive where it is warm and dry; others prefer wet or moist conditions. Some are influenced by cycles of drought. Degrees of shade or sunlight, slope, and soil type can also influence pest establishment. Pests are often first found in certain spots, such as at the edges of a lawn, rather than distributed evenly throughout the turf.

Diagnosing the Problem

In trying to discover the source of lawn damage, the easiest and most reliable method is to look closely. Chances are you can see the pests in action. Simply get down on your hands and knees, part the grass with your fingers, and concentrate your attention on the edge of a damaged area. Like fungi, insects tend to proceed with their damage from a central point outward; they are most active on the outside edge, where the damaged area meets the healthy grass. Part the leaves and look into the thatch layer. Focus on a specific area for several seconds and watch for insect movements. Look for evidence of pest infestation such as green, pellet-shaped droppings left by sod webworms.

Flea beetles, leafhoppers, scale insects, and spider mites can be found, if present, by carefully examining the leaves, stems, and crowns of grasses. Chinch bugs can be found by looking closely in these areas and among any thatch.

Cutworms, fiery skipper larvae, and sod webworms, which live near or under the soil, can be detected by a procedure called the pyrethrum test. Mix 1 tablespoonful of commercial garden pesticide containing 1 to 2 percent pyrethrum (a natural insect poison produced by plants) in 1 gallon of water. Mark off 1 square yard of lawn area, including some damaged and some undamaged grass, and apply the entire gallon mixture as evenly as possible to that area with a sprinkling can. Deadly at normal doses, the diluted pyrethrum is irritating to many insects. Within a few minutes they will come to the surface where you can see them.

If no pyrethrum is available, you can obtain similar results by flooding the area with soapy water. Place the end of a garden hose on the area to be checked and let the water run for 5 to 10 minutes. Any insects will soon surface. Several areas of the lawn should be checked to determine the extent of an infestation.

Neither white grubs nor billbug larvae will respond to the pyrethrum test or to flooding. Instead, carefully dig around the roots of grass in an area of 1 to 2 square feet. If infestations of grubs are heavy, grass roots will be eaten away and the grass can be rolled back like a carpet. Grass plants damaged by billbug larvae will pull out at their crowns, exposing a sawdustlike material. If more than about 5 cutworms, 10 skipper larvae, or 15 sod webworms appear on average per square yard, or if more than 6 white grub or billbug larvae are found per square foot, control measures should be taken.

No measures will be necessary for many of the creatures you will find, since they are not pests; it is therefore essential to identify all suspects correctly before you apply any treatment.

Treating the Problem

Some of the symptoms you will find in a lawn, such as withering, browning, or yellowing of leaf blades, may be caused by diseases or unfavorable soil conditions. They may also be caused by inadequate watering or fertilizing, poor drainage, or too much shade. Investigate these possibilities before taking any pest control measures.

Cultural controls The first line of defense against lawn pests is to select the right grass for your situation and to maintain it properly. Poorly adapted, poorly kept lawns show pest injury sooner and recover more slowly than vigorous, well-kept lawns.

Lawns are especially vulnerable to insect attacks while they are becoming established. Amend the soil before planting, and keep it fertilized to enhance healthy growth. Keep the lawn weed free. Insects may first be attracted to weeds, then move on to the grass.

Allowing thatch to accumulate can greatly increase the damage insects cause. Thatch provides insects with an ideal place in which to live and reproduce. Any insecticides applied to the

If grubs are numerous, grass roots will be eaten away and the turf can be lifted up easily. Grubs (beetle larvae) are among the few insects that can damage a lawn to this extent.

Using a Pesticide

Pesticides should always be used with care and deliberation. Here are some important cautions regarding their use.

• Use a pesticide only when a definite need has been established, since these chemicals are toxic. Most of them can harm beneficial bees and wildlife along with the pests that damage lawns. Some of them also slow down grass seed germination and the growth of new seedlings or sod. Overuse can also increase pesticide resistance in the pests you are attempting to kill.

• Do not mix pesticides together, or with other lawn chemicals, unless their labels state that this is permissible. Doing so may make them more toxic, less effective, or both. Many pesticides cannot be mixed with lime, iron, or copper, because reactions with these elements can make the product toxic to plants. They also may be physically incompatible, causing the sprayer to clog.

• Keep pesticides away from streams and other water supplies. Toxic chemicals are becoming increasingly common in these environments.

• Keep children and pets off a treated lawn until the pesticide on the grass has dried. This normally takes a few hours, but it may take somewhat longer if the weather is damp.

• Avoid spraying on a windy day. If pesticides land on automobiles, wash them off immediately. Some chemicals may cause spotting on automobile finishes.

• Do not mow the lawn for at least 24 hours after a pesticide has been applied. This gives the material time to begin taking effect.

• Do not spray pesticides when the temperature exceeds 85° F. Rapid evaporation at these temperatures makes the pesticides more concentrated and thus more likely to burn the grass. (Temperature is less critical with granular pesticides.)

• Store chemicals out of the reach of children, in their original labeled containers. It is best to keep them out of sunlight in a cool place, if possible in a locked enclosure.

lawn become bound to the organic matter in the thatch and cannot move efficiently into the soil, where more insects or larvae may be hiding. Thatch buildup also keeps water and air from penetrating the soil, weakening the grass and making it more susceptible to insect damage. All these are good reasons to keep thatch from building up in your lawn. For a guide to routine thatch removal, see pages 76 and 77.

Chemical and biological controls Pesticides are not the only solutions to lawn pest problems. But if you decide they are necessary, they can be an effective way of ridding your lawn of insects.

Pesticides for lawns are applied in two forms: sprays and granules. Most sprays work very quickly, killing many insects in the first 48 hours. They are typically applied to the lawn with a hose-end sprayer, which uses water pressure from a garden hose to disperse concentrated pesticide.

Granular materials consist of inert carriers such as clay, vermiculite, or corncob particles that are coated with pesticide. They are usually spread over the lawn with a broadcaster or drop spreader. The granules release the pesticide gradually as they absorb moisture. Granular materials usually last longer than sprays, but sprays are more effective for killing insects that feed on the aboveground portions of the grass.

Pesticides are further classified as contact or systemic. Contact pesticides kill when pests touch them or are touched by them. Systemic pesticides are absorbed by plants internally; pests are poisoned as they feed on various plant parts. Some pesticides kill both systemically and on contact. The drawback of contact insecticides is that they are easily removed by rain, watering, or mowing; however, there may be no other effective control for the pest you are trying to eradicate. The drawback of systemics is that they do not always work as quickly as contact products. The most complete information on pest control products is on the product labels. Always read the label before purchasing a product.

In most cases, pesticides should be applied only when pests are present in sufficient numbers to cause damage. The ideal time to spray on contact pesticides is in late afternoon or early evening, since most of the pests that attack the leaves and stems of grasses feed at night. The spray will either kill the insects by direct contact or brush onto them as they move about the foliage and thatch. Granular pesticides or systemic sprays can be applied at any time of day unless it is hot. Applying them in hot weather can damage the grass.

Lawns being treated with sprays or granules for an aboveground infestation should first be watered well, since drought-stressed grasses can be damaged by these chemicals. Water the lawn one or two days before treatment and apply the pesticide as soon as the lawn dries. Then withhold further watering for 48 hours unless the label indicates otherwise. This delay lets the pesticide remain on the plants for as long as possible, maximizing its effectiveness.

If your spraying is targeted at underground pests, water the lawn immediately after you spray. This will carry the pesticide off the foliage and down through the thatch to where the insects are. If the soil is dry, watering it before you spray helps the insecticide move down to where the grubs are feeding.

Unless the label indicates otherwise, granular pesticides are best applied when the lawn is wet, since they are activated by moisture. Granular materials will also stick better to wet grass.

Insects usually do their worst damage during the summer months, because that is when the populations of many species are largest. Grass has often been weakened by summer heat and drought and is thus more likely to succumb to insect injury. This damage is often compounded because homeowners mistake the insect damage for normal summer dormancy. It is important to look closely at the damaged grass to determine whether insects are indeed the problem. In most cases the culprits will be readily visible.

Insect pests that live and feed in the soil are harder to control than aboveground pests because pesticides cannot be applied to them directly. In order to make contact, the chemical must penetrate the thatch and move down to the soil or plant parts where the insects are. The thicker the thatch, the longer this takes. Shorter-term pesticides may lose much of their toxicity before they reach their targets. If your lawn is thick with thatch, either remove the thatch or treat the lawn with a more persistent pesticide such as isofenphos.

It is important to recognize that some pests will survive a pesticide application. The survivors are usually not numerous enough to present an immediate threat, but when they reproduce, their populations may again build up to injurious levels. Retreatment may eventually become necessary. It is also a good idea to vary the pesticides you use during the year; if you use the same pesticide repeatedly, insect populations may grow resistant to it over time.

Identifying the Pest

The following are descriptions of pests that can do significant damage to lawns, as well as those that harm lawns only occasionally or in confined regions. Some are large and easy to detect; others are identified mainly by the type of damage they do.

When contemplating the use of a pesticide it is essential to know what you are dealing with, since controls vary in effectiveness against different pests. Also, some pests are much less devastating than others. Depending on the degree of damage you can tolerate, you may feel that you would rather live with a pest than use a pesticide.

Note that the chemicals named here are active ingredients that may be found in more than one product. Your local garden center can guide you to products containing the ingredients you need. Because the list of approved pesticides changes periodically, check with your garden center or agricultural extension service for the latest information.

Armyworms, cutworms, and fiery skippers These three moth larvae chew off the grass blades above the soil surface. If there are many of them, the grass is eaten to the soil level. The damage they cause is similar to that of sod webworms.

Armyworm caterpillars are light tan to dark brown with yellow, orange, or dark brown stripes down the lengths of their backs. They are ¾ inch to 2 inches long. Adult moths (which do not harm lawns) are tan or mottled gray with a wingspan of about 1 inch. They fly only at night.

Cutworms are plump, smooth, and almost always curl up when disturbed. They can be various colors but are most often gray, brown, or black; some are spotted or striped. They are stout creatures, often growing to 2 inches long.

Fiery skippers are about 1 inch long and brownish yellow, with dark brown heads and thin necks. They are usually a minor problem but can be serious pests of bentgrass and bermudagrass lawns, especially hybrid bermudagrass. They can also be a problem for bluegrass lawns in some areas.

Use the pyrethrum test (see page 90) to determine how pervasive these insects are. If you find five or more per square yard, treat with products containing chlorpyrifos, diazinon, Orthene®, or Sevin®.

Bermudagrass mites Bermudagrass mites suck juices from plants. Heavily infested grass

Armyworms, Cutworms, and Fiery Skippers

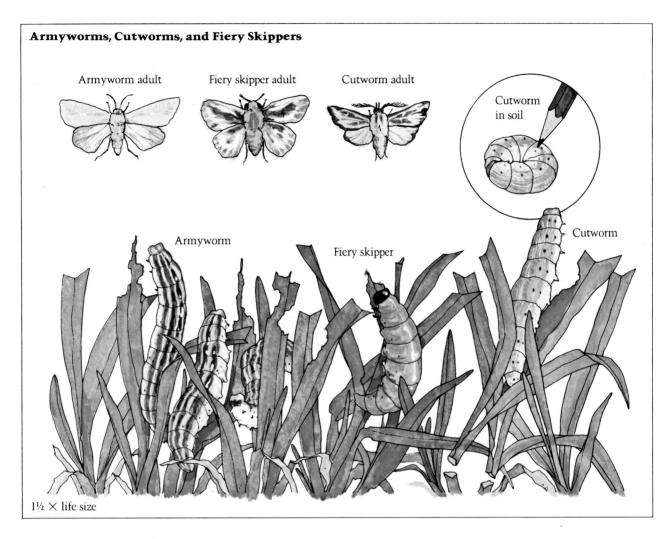

Armyworm adult   Fiery skipper adult   Cutworm adult

Cutworm in soil

Cutworm

Armyworm

Fiery skipper

1½ × life size

takes on a brown, dry appearance, and new growth is retarded.

Female mites lay eggs under the leaf sheaths. The eggs soon hatch and many mites begin feeding on the stems and in protected areas of the leaf sheaths.

Close examination of infested grass plants will reveal a whitish, moldy material on the stems and crown. These are the mites. You can sometimes isolate bermudagrass mites by shaking infested grass over white paper. Control by thatch removal, or use diazinon.

Billbugs   A small and distinct circular pattern becomes yellowish or brown when billbugs are a problem in the lawn. Since the larvae feed on stems, grass stems within the dead areas lift easily out of the soil. A whitish sawdustlike debris can be found on the ground.

Billbug larvae are white, legless grubs about ⅜ inch long. The adults are ¼ to ¾ inches long, with snouts that are used for burrowing and chewing off plants.

Adults spend winter in or near an infested area. In spring they can be seen crawling on sidewalks and driveways. They lay eggs above the crowns of grass plants. Larvae feed and tunnel into the stems, eventually migrating into the root zone.

To check for billbug larvae, dig in the edges of brown areas near green, healthy grass. Examine the soil around the grass roots. If, on average, more than one grub is found per square foot, treat the lawn with an insecticide such as chlorpyrifos, diazinon, or isofenphos in midsummer. Control adult beetles by placing any of these insecticides on grass foliage and thatch in spring, when adults are moving about.

Different species of billbugs prefer different types of grass. In southern areas, bermudagrass and zoysiagrass are commonly attacked; in the north, Kentucky bluegrass is preferred. Most damage is caused in midsummer.

Chinch bugs   When chinch bugs are present, you will see large, distinct, circular patches.

Billbugs

Adult

Larva

2½ × life size

Bermudagrass Mites

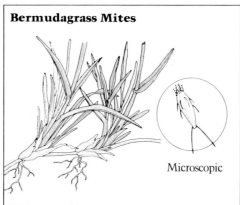

Microscopic

Chinch Bugs

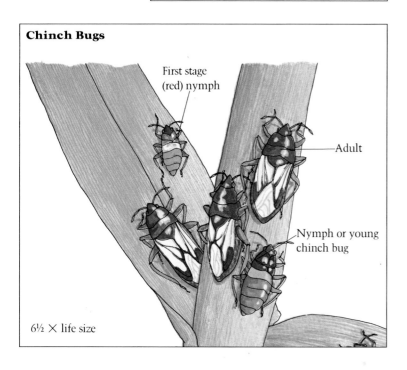

First stage
(red) nymph

Adult

Nymph or young
chinch bug

6½ × life size

They are most often a problem in centipede-grass, fine fescue, and St. Augustine grass, but creeping bentgrass, Kentucky bluegrass, and zoysiagrass may be affected. The yellowish spots are confined to sunny areas of the lawn and look browner toward the center.

Chinch bugs crawl down into the leaves and stems and suck the juices from grass blades. They also inject a poison that causes blades to turn brown and die. They congregate where the grass is just beginning to turn yellow, rather than in dead or green areas. They will continue to move outward toward healthy green grass in ever-widening circles. They thrive in hot, dry weather. To check for chinch bugs, push a bottomless metal can into the affected lawn area and fill it with warm water. Any chinch bugs should float to the surface.

Chinch bugs are quite small, with adults ranging from $\frac{1}{16}$ to $\frac{1}{4}$ inch long, depending on the species. Most are black with white wings, each of which has a distinctive triangular black mark. Young chinch bugs look like smaller, wingless versions of their parents, but they are red with a white back stripe.

To help control chinch bugs, grow resistant 'Floratam' St. Augustine grass, or use chlorpyrifos, diazinon, or isofenphos.

Clover mites You may first become aware of these pests when they move inside your house looking for a warm place to spend the winter. They live primarily on clover and similar plants in the lawn, sucking out the plant juices. This feeding gives the lawn a silvery appearance. Damage is most serious in areas close to buildings or planter boxes.

Clover mites are tiny ($\frac{1}{30}$ inch) green to red-brown spiders that live and feed on the undersurface of grass blades. When crushed, the mites leave a red stain. Sometimes their webbing is visible.

These pests are usually kept in check by predatory insects, or chemical treatments for other pests. If treatment is necessary, use diazinon, chlorpyrifos, malathion, or dicofol (a miticide), as the label directs.

Crane flies A lawn bothered by crane flies loses patches of grass, often beginning at the edge of the lawn. When an area is heavily infested, you will see a brownish paste covering the soil over the missing grass. Brownish gray grubs, about an inch long, may be found on top of and just below the soil surface.

Adult crane flies look similar to mosquitoes, except that they are much larger and do not bite. The adults do not damage the lawn, but they do lay eggs in lawns in late summer. The grubs that hatch (called leatherjackets) are slender and about 2 inches long. They damage a lawn by feeding on grass blades, and the worst damage occurs in spring.

Use a product containing chlorpyrifos or diazinon when damage first appears. Treatment is most effective in spring.

Greenbugs Rust-colored patches of grass appear under trees when greenbugs are present. These patches of grass turn brown and die, and the damage then spreads to the sunny parts of the lawn. Grass blades may have yellow to rust-colored spots with dark centers.

Greenbugs are tiny aphids that suck sap from and inject a poison into grass blades. They can kill an entire lawn if left uncontrolled. Underwatered or overfertilized Kentucky bluegrass lawns are particularly susceptible to greenbugs. Damage occurs primarily after mild winters and cool springs.

At the first sign of damage, spray the lawn with a product containing Orthene®, and repeat if the symptoms continue. Follow proper watering and fertilizing guidelines.

Ground pearls Ground pearls are tiny scale insects that attack the roots of bermudagrass and centipedegrass, mostly in the southern and southwestern states. By feeding on plant juices in the root zone, the ⅛-inch ground pearls cause grass to turn brown and eventually die in late summer, leaving irregular brown patches. Damage occurs more in sandy soils than in clay soils. Prevent by keeping the lawn well fertilized, watered, and mowed. Chemical control is usually not needed.

Grubs Grubs are the larvae of many kinds of beetles. Most are whitish or grayish with brown heads and dark hind parts, and measure 1 to 1½ inches long when fully grown. They have three pairs of legs, which distinguishes them from the legless billbug grubs. They are usually curled in a C shape. The adult beetles appear around the garden in late spring or summer. Grubs feed beneath the soil on the

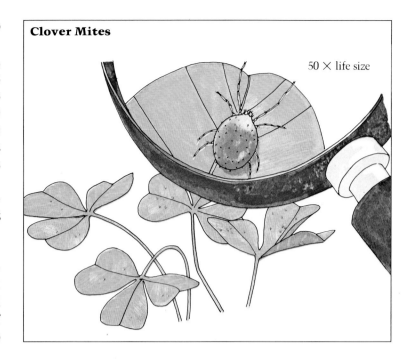

Clover Mites

50 × life size

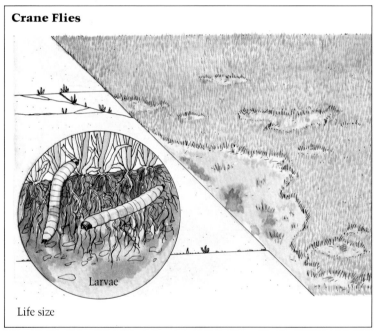

Crane Flies

Larvae

Life size

roots of grasses. For signs of grub activity, look for irregularly shaped brown patches in late spring or early fall. Dead patches of lawn roll back easily, like a section of carpet. Birds, moles, raccoons, and skunks may damage a lawn looking for grubs.

If you find six or more grubs per square foot of exposed soil, your lawn is infested. To control grubs, use a product containing chlorpyrifos, diazinon, isofenphos, or trichlorfon. Repeated heavy waterings are needed after application to carry the pesticide down through grass and thatch into the soil.

Greenbugs

10 × life size

Ground Pearls

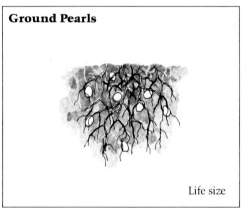

Life size

Grubs

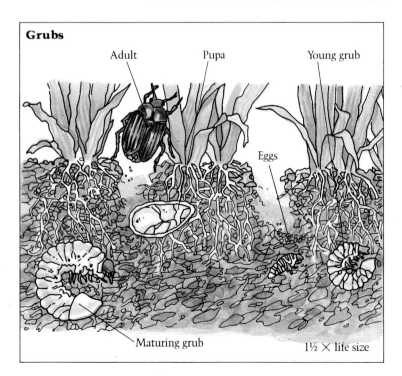

Adult   Pupa   Young grub

Eggs

Maturing grub   1½ × life size

Mole crickets   Mole crickets are burrowing relatives of the jumping type that are found in such warm-season grasses as bahiagrass, bermudagrass, centipedegrass, St. Augustine grass, and sometimes zoysiagrass. They cause irregular streaks of brown and wilted grass. The dead grass pulls up easily, and you can find the crickets' tunnels with your fingers or even see them if the ground is bare.

Mole crickets are about 1½ to 2 inches long and brown or grayish brown. They look similar to the common cricket, except that their heads and their front legs are notably large. They feed on grass roots and, by their tunneling, cause nearby roots to dry out.

The most common control is a mole cricket bait containing chlorpyrifos. Apply the bait in the evening before a warm night, watering the lawn first. Diazinon, isofenphos, chlorpyrifos, or Orthene® can also be used in spring about a week after the first signs of mole cricket activity appear.

Moles and gophers   Moles and gophers are rodents that live underground. Moles feed on earthworms, grubs, and other insects; gophers eat plant roots or entire plants. Each causes damage to the lawn by severing grass roots, raising sod, and, in the case of gophers, eating sections of the lawn.

When moles are present, you will notice raised ridges, 3 to 5 inches wide, on the lawn. These ridges sometimes turn brown. Gophers create crescent-shaped mounds of soil on the lawn. On close probing, you will find a hole underneath each mound. Gophers are found primarily in western regions.

Trapping or baiting is the best way to eliminate gophers from your yard. For serious problems, a licensed professional can fill holes and tunnels with special pellets that release a poisonous gas when moistened. Moles are harder to control with traps or poisons because of the fragile, temporary nature of their surface tunnels. One way to help rid your lawn of moles is to eliminate grubs, a favorite food.

Nematodes   Nematodes are small worms that are common in the soil. They are so small that you need a microscope to see them, but scientists say they are the most common form of life on earth. There are thousands of different kinds, but only a few damage plants.

When harmful nematodes are present in a lawn, the grass is slow growing, thin, yellowish, and especially susceptible to summer drought. The roots are stubby and shallow, possibly showing swellings or galls. The lawn will not respond to treatments such as aeration, fertilization, or watering. Complete diagnosis requires a professional laboratory analysis.

To control harmful nematodes, keep the grass as healthy as possible. If the presence of damaging nematodes is confirmed by a professional, consult an experienced pest control operator or your county extension agent.

Sod webworms The adult form of the webworm is a buff-colored moth that flies in a zigzag pattern just a few feet above the lawn. The moths themselves do not damage the lawn; rather, they drop eggs into the grass that, on hatching, develop into hungry caterpillars.

Sod webworms feed at night. They chew grass blades off just above the thatch line and pull the blades into a silken tunnel to eat them. In late spring or summer, the feeding larvae create small 1- to 2-inch dead patches amid normal grass. Sod webworms hide during the day in shelters constructed of bits of grass and debris. Break apart damaged areas to check for them. Look for slender, grayish, black-spotted caterpillars, to about ¾ inch long, that are rather sluggish in their activity. Other evidence of their presence is their green-tan excrement. Birds and moles feeding on the lawn may indicate a large population. If you find 15

Mole Crickets

1⅓ × life size

Moles and Gophers

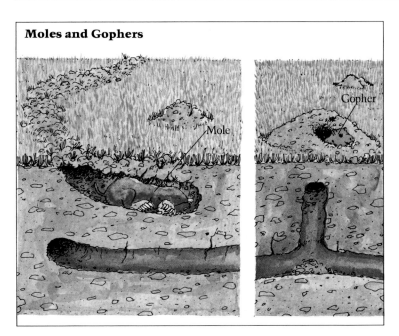

Mole

Gopher

Sod Webworms

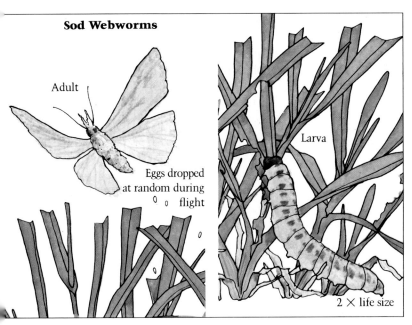

Adult

Eggs dropped at random during flight

Larva

2 × life size

Nematodes

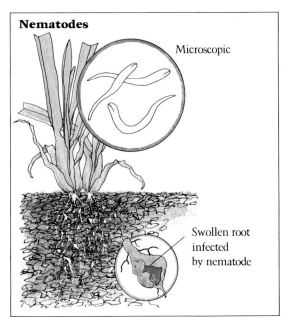

Microscopic

Swollen root infected by nematode

or more worms per square foot, consider using a pesticide.

To control, use a product containing chlorpyrifos, diazinon, isofenphos, Orthene®, Sevin®, or trichlorfon. Removing thatch will make the lawn less desirable to webworms.

DISEASES

Most lawn diseases are caused by parasitic plants called fungi, which spread by microscopic spores. Most fungi grow best under cool, moist conditions. If allowed to gain a foothold, some can be quite damaging to lawns.

Fungal diseases are easier to prevent than to cure. Planting the right kind of grass for your climate will go a long way toward minimizing the chance of disease; poorly adapted grasses are weaker and more susceptible to attack. Watering in the morning rather than at night can also retard fungal growth by allowing the lawn to dry out during the day.

If fungal diseases do take hold, they can usually be controlled with fungicides. These products are most effective if applied before the disease becomes severe.

Fungicides

To prevent and control diseases caused by fungi, a number of fungicides are commonly used on home lawns. These are categorized as either contact or systemic. Contact fungicides work on the outside of plants. They are best used before diseases start. For example, if you know from past experience that a particular disease attacks your lawn at a certain time of year, prevent the disease by applying the appropriate fungicide two weeks beforehand.

Systemic fungicides work from inside plants and are usually the most effective. However, some systemic fungicides are specific and only control certain diseases.

Both contact and systemic fungicides are sold in several forms: as granules that are spread over the lawn, as powders that are mixed with water for spraying, and as "flowables" or liquids that can be sprayed. Granules tend to be easier to apply, and most remain on the lawn longer than sprays, prolonging their effectiveness. Some chemicals remain effective longer than others, but most usually work for up to two weeks. Check the label for exact information.

In general, fungal diseases are more difficult to control with chemicals than are insects, simply because of the way in which fungi grow in the infected plants. They are able to penetrate the plant and proliferate there, which makes them hard to reach. If accidentally ingested, most fungicides are much less toxic to animals than pesticides. However, many fungicides produce skin irritations. Like pesticides, they should be handled and used with great care. Always study the product label thoroughly, especially for rates and timing.

Lawn Diseases

The control of lawn diseases should begin with a rapid and accurate diagnosis of the problem. This diagnosis is often based on knowledge of the weaknesses and susceptibilities of your particular grass. Once you have eliminated insects or cultural problems as causes of the symptoms you are seeing, consider a disease as the source.

Lawn diseases vary in severity from year to year and from place to place, depending on weather conditions, lawn care patterns, and the ecology of the disease organisms themselves. Some are active at certain seasons; others can strike at any time. The following pages describe the most common lawn diseases and give advice on how to control them.

Note that the chemicals named here are active ingredients that may be found in more than one product. Your local garden center can guide you to products containing the ingredients you need. Because the list of approved fungicides changes periodically, check with your garden center or agricultural extension service for the latest information.

Brown Patch (Rhizoctonia Blight)
Mid to late summer
A serious disease in the South on centipedegrass and St. Augustine grass, this fungus also attacks bentgrass, bermudagrass, rough bluegrass, fescue, ryegrass, and zoysiagrass.

Brown patch is recognized by large, irregular, circular areas from 6 inches to several feet in diameter. The center of a spot may recover, resulting in a ring of diseased grass. The patches usually have a brown to gray discoloration, with a water-soaked appearance around the edges of the patch. Brown patch usually attacks only leaves and stems.

High summer temperatures (75° to 95° F), excessive thatch, high humidity, lush growth

Brown Patch

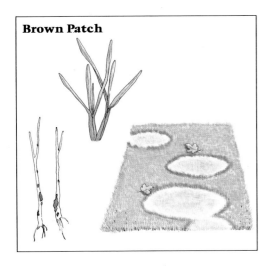

Damping-Off

Dollar Spot

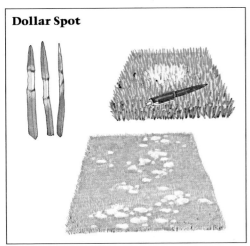

Fairy Ring

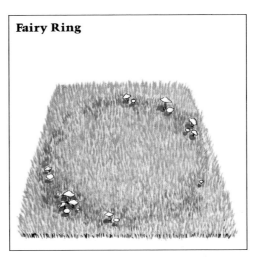

from overfertilizing, and excessive moisture create perfect conditions for this disease.

To prevent brown patch, avoid heavy doses of nitrogen fertilizer, reduce shade and thatch, water deeply when necessary, and keep the lawn aerated. To treat, apply anilazine, chlorothalonil, fenarimol, iprodione, maneb, PCNB, thiram, or triadimefon.

Some improved varieties of Kentucky bluegrass resist this disease.

Damping-Off

Seedling lawns

When new seedlings fail to fill in properly, damping-off disease may be present. Look closely to see whether young seedlings have emerged from the soil but collapsed.

Damping-off is caused by a number of fungal organisms. The condition most favorable to these organisms is overwatering after seeding, especially if the soil is heavy and the days are overcast. Other contributing factors may be excessive nitrogen or overly deep sowing of seeds.

Prevent damping-off by using seeds treated with captan or thiram; or spray captan, chloroneb, ethazol, metalaxyl, or thiram on newly seeded areas. Fumigating the soil prior to planting is another preventive method.

Damping-off can strike any seeded grass, but it is not a problem in lawns started from sprigs or plugs.

Dollar Spot

Spring to fall

This common fungal disease attacks several types of grass including Kentucky bluegrass, fescue, and ryegrass, but it is the most severe in bentgrass and bermudagrass. It kills in small spots, about 2 inches in diameter, but the spots may fuse into large, irregular areas that may girdle the leaves. Diseased spots usually range from tan to straw colored. Fine, white, cobwebby fungus threads may be seen in early morning on the infected grass.

Dollar spot is common near foggy coasts, especially in bentgrass lawns. Moderate temperatures

Fusarium Patch

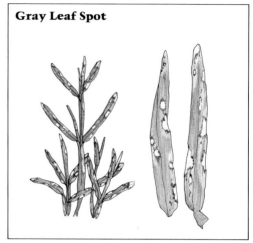

Gray Leaf Spot

(60° to 80° F), excess moisture, and excess thatch all favor it. Nitrogen-deficient lawns develop more dollar spot than those that are fertilized adequately.

To keep dollar spot from taking hold, increase applications of nitrogen fertilizer, keep thatch at a minimum, and water deeply when necessary (but avoid watering in the evening). Chemical controls include anilazine, chlorothalonil, fenarimol, iprodione, thiophanate, and triadimefon.

Some of the new, improved cultivars of Kentucky bluegrass, fine fescue, and perennial ryegrass can resist this disease.

Fairy Ring
Spring to fall
This fungal disease appears as rings of dark green grass surrounding areas of dead or light-colored grass. Grass inside the ring dies because water cannot penetrate the cobwebby surface of the fungus, which lies near the top of the soil. After prolonged wet weather, mushrooms (the fruiting bodies of the fungus) may appear around the edge of the ring, where the fungus is actively growing. More than fifty kinds of fungus can produce a fairy ring.

Fairy ring develops in soils that contain undecomposed, woody organic matter, such as dead tree roots or old construction materials. It can affect all types of grass, but the effects may be less severe in grass varieties with long stolons.

Try to keep the lawn growing by applying adequate nitrogen fertilizer to hide the problem. Aerate rings and use a wetting agent to improve water penetration. Keep areas wet for about two weeks and mow frequently. If you cannot stand the sight, you can also dig up the

entire area of a ring to a depth of 12 inches, and replace it with fresh soil and new seed, sod, sprigs, or plugs.

It is difficult to eradicate fairy ring with a fungicide. The lawn can be fumigated with methyl bromide, but this kills the grass and must be applied by a licensed professional. It is best to try to live with this disease.

Fusarium Patch
Fall to spring
Also called pink snow mold, this fungal disease develops under snow or at the margins of a melting snow bank. It can also appear in the absence of snow. The disease appears as roughly circular dead patches 1 to 2 inches in diameter, which may enlarge to 12 inches. Leaves first become water soaked and then turn reddish brown, then bleached. Small white or pinkish gel-like spore masses are occasionally seen on dead leaves. Fungus threads, also white or pinkish, may be seen in early morning.

Look for fusarium patch on annual bluegrass and common Kentucky bluegrass, creeping bentgrass, fescue, ryegrass, and zoysiagrass. It thrives best in cool (40° to 50° F), moist conditions.

Reducing shade, improving soil aeration and drainage, and avoiding excess fall fertilizing with nitrogen can keep fusarium patch from becoming a problem. Removing thatch buildup also helps.

To treat the disease, apply fenarimol, iprodione, or triadimefon. Fungicides are more effective if applied late in fall, before the disease develops.

Some improved varieties of Kentucky bluegrass resist fusarium patch.

Gray Leaf Spot

Mid to late summer

Gray leaf spot attacks St. Augustine grass, especially in recently sprigged or plugged lawns. The spots on the grass blades are ash to brown in color and surrounded by a brown to purple margin. The yellowing turf looks drought stricken. At the worst stages of this fungal disease, blades scorch or die back.

The disease occurs during periods of high humidity and high nitrogen fertilization, especially when temperatures range between 80° and 90° F. There have been some reports of damage to bermudagrass, centipedegrass, fescue, and ryegrass.

To help prevent gray leaf spot, do not overfertilize with nitrogen. Water as infrequently as the lawn tolerates. When you do water, do so in the morning and be sure the moisture penetrates to at least 5 inches. Prune shade trees, if possible, to increase light and air circulation.

To control infestations, apply anilazine, captan, chlorothalonil, maneb, or PCNB.

'Roselawn' and 'Tamlawn' St. Augustine grass have shown resistance.

Leaf Spot

Spring to fall

Leaf spot, also known as melting out, refers to a family of fungal diseases (the drechslera diseases) that favor bermudagrass, Kentucky bluegrass, and fescue. Its most obvious symptoms are elongated, circular spots on grass blades. These spots have brown or straw-colored centers with black to purplish borders.

Cool (50° to 70° F), moist conditions are the most favorable to leaf spot. It first appears in the shade and is the most severe in closely mowed lawns. The Kentucky bluegrass varieties 'Delta', 'Kenblue', and 'Park' are the most susceptible.

To prevent the organisms from growing, reduce the amount of shade, improve aeration and drainage, and mow at the recommended height. Do not overfertilize in spring. Water deeply in the morning.

For control, apply anilazine, captan, chlorothalonil, iprodione, maneb, PCNB, thiophanate, or zineb.

The most resistant grasses are 'Adelphi', 'Challenger', 'Eclipse', 'Midnight', and other Kentucky bluegrasses.

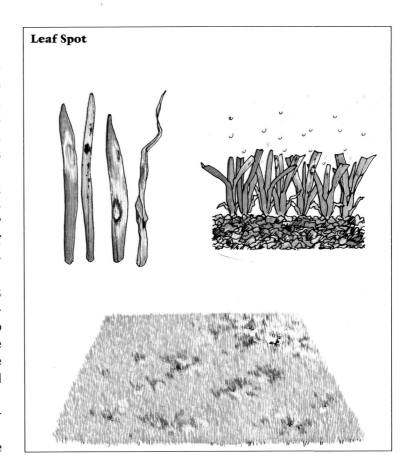

Leaf Spot

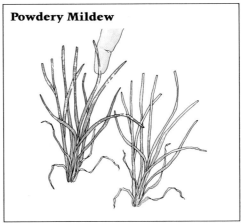

Powdery Mildew

Powdery Mildew

Midsummer to fall

The first symptoms of powdery mildew are light patches of dusty white to light gray on grass blades. Lower leaves may become completely covered. Although it is usually not too serious a problem, coverage can be severe. When the growth becomes dense, the infected areas look as though lime has just been spread or the area has been lightly sprayed with white paint. It commonly occurs in shady areas.

Slow or nonexistent air circulation, shade, and high humidity with temperatures of 60° to

Pythium Blight

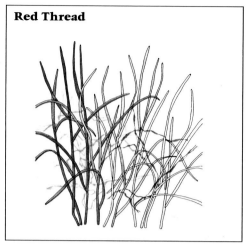

Red Thread

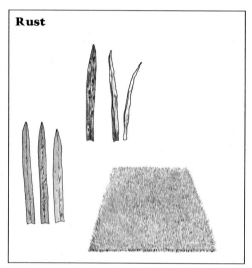

Rust

St. Augustine Grass Decline (SAD)

70° F are the most common contributors to this disease. Bermudagrass, Kentucky bluegrass, and zoysiagrass are its most frequent victims.

To prevent powdery mildew, plant shade-tolerant grasses. The most resistant of these are 'Birka', 'Bristol', 'Glade', and 'Nugget' Kentucky bluegrass; and 'Aurora', 'Flyer', 'Fortress', 'Reliant', and 'Shadow' fine fescue. For cultural control, avoid excessive nitrogen fertilization and herbicide applications in shade. Mow the lawn high. Use selective pruning to increase air circulation and admit more sun.

To control an outbreak, apply fenarimol or triadimefon.

Pythium Blight
Late summer
This fungal disease, also known as cottony blight or grease spot, usually occurs only on newly established lawns. However, it can be a problem in any lawn when temperatures are high and excess moisture is present.

The first indication of this disease is the appearance of irregular patches a few inches in diameter. (On closely cut lawns, these frequently appear as circular spots about 2 inches across.) The grass leaves appear water soaked, soft and slimy, thus the name grease spot. The blades soon wither and fade to light brown or straw color, sometimes reddish brown, particularly if the weather is sunny and windy. Then the patches join to form large damaged areas often several feet in diameter. These assume various shapes sometimes corresponding to the drainage pattern. The white, cottony fungus can be seen on the leaves of diseased plants in the early morning.

The most susceptible grasses are bentgrass, bermudagrass, Kentucky bluegrass, turf-type tall fescue, and annual ryegrass (especially when it is used for overseeding in the South). There are no resistant varieties.

To help prevent pythium blight, avoid overwatering, especially in newly seeded areas.

Make sure the new lawn has good drainage. Use only treated seeds, and do not sow them more thickly than is recommended on the label. In established lawns, water in the morning and avoid mowing wet grass in hot weather.

For chemical control, use chloroneb, metalaxyl, or propamocarb hydrochloride when the symptoms first appear.

Red Thread
Fall

Also known as pink patch, this disease is common in the Pacific Northwest and the Northeast. The first and least obvious symptom is small spots that appear water soaked; these enlarge rapidly and cover a large part of the leaf. As the spots dry out, the leaves fade to a light brown or tan. At later stages the fungus forms thin, red to pink fingerlike structures—the "red threads"—at the tips of grass leaves. These give the lawn a reddish cast.

This distinctive fungus is most damaging in spring and fall when temperatures range from 68° to 75° F and humidity is high. Kentucky bluegrass, red fescue, ryegrass, and sometimes bentgrass are frequent targets.

To help prevent red thread, maintain an adequate nitrogen level and a soil pH of 6.5 to 7.0. Water deeply in the morning.

Apply anilazine, chlorothalonil, iprodione, or triadimefon to help control the disease.

Many improved cultivars of Kentucky bluegrass and hard fescue resist red thread.

Rust
Midsummer to fall

True to its name, this fungal disease gives infected lawns a rust-colored cast that is noticeable from a distance. The dustlike rust spores, which are the main symptom of this disease, form in circular or elongated groups on grass blades. If the infection is severe, anything moving through the area—such as shoes, clothing, or lawn equipment—will be covered by the spores and potentially spread the disease.

Rust proliferates in moderately warm, moist weather. Dew remaining on plants for 10 to 12 hours is enough to promote germination of the fungus spores, particularly on underfertilized lawns. Spores range in color from chestnut brown to orange and yellow, emerging from pustules on the leaf blades. Rust affects almost all commonly grown grasses, but Kentucky bluegrass and annual ryegrass are damaged most frequently.

To help prevent rust, make the lawn grow rapidly by fertilizing with nitrogen and watering frequently. The growth of the grass blades pushes the rust-infected leaves upward, where they can be mowed off and removed. Better yet, grow grasses that are resistant to the disease. Among these are fine fescues, new cultivars of Kentucky bluegrass, and perennial ryegrass.

Chemical treatment is necessary only in severe cases. Use anilazine, chlorothalonil, maneb, triadimefon, or zineb.

St. Augustine Grass Decline (SAD)
Anytime

Known to occur only in Texas and Louisiana, SAD is a virus that attacks only St. Augustine grass. The earliest symptoms are pale green or yellowish spots, blotches, and a speckling or stippling of the leaves. These are followed by overall yellowing, stunted growth, and a general decline in vigor. A St. Augustine grass lawn attacked by SAD is usually invaded by bermudagrass and weeds, which are not affected by the disease.

The only control is to plant plugs of resistant grasses into the middle of the infested areas. These eventually replace the diseased grass. Some varieties of St. Augustine grass are resistant to SAD. These include 'Floralawn', 'Floratam', 'Raleigh', 'Seville', and 'Tamlawn'. Take care to prevent spread of the virus in leaf clippings and mowing equipment.

Stripe Smut
Spring to fall

Grasses infected with stripe smut fungus are usually pale green and stunted. Stripes or streaks of spore masses form along the surface of the grass blades, turning from light to dark. Affected blades curl, die, and become shredded by the advancing disease.

The moderate temperatures of spring and fall encourage stripe smut, which most commonly attacks bentgrass and Kentucky bluegrass. Hot, dry weather often halts it.

To help prevent infection, keep thatch to a minimum, reduce fertilizer applications, and avoid overwatering. Use seed treated with fungicides. Some of the numerous varieties of Kentucky bluegrass that resist the disease are

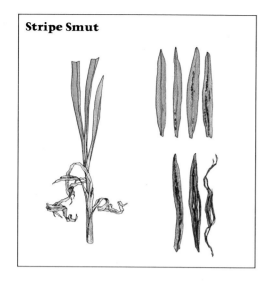

Stripe Smut

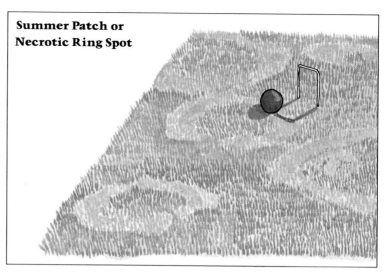

**Summer Patch or
Necrotic Ring Spot**

'Adelphi', 'A-34' (also known as 'Bensun'), and 'Sydsport'.

Chemical controls are best applied in late fall. Fenarimol, PCNB, or triadimefon provide some control.

Summer Patch
Midsummer
Formerly called fusarium blight, summer patch begins as scattered light green patches up to 8 inches in diameter that turn dull tan to reddish brown. Of the larger diseased patches in the lawn, the easiest to recognize is the "frog-eye" pattern—an apparently healthy green patch of grass that is partially or completely surrounded by a ring of dead grass.

Hot, dry, and windy weather creates an excellent climate for this fungal disease. Summer patch most often occurs when hot (83° to 89° F), sunny days follow warm periods that have alternated between wet and dry. Grasses most susceptible to summer patch include bentgrass, 'Fylking' and 'Park' Kentucky bluegrass, new cultivars of turf-type tall fescue, and perennial ryegrass.

To help control summer patch, aerate the lawn to improve root growth. Fertilize with nitrogen, but take care not to use too much. Follow correct mowing and watering practices. Light, frequent watering helps during drought. Planting a mixture of Kentucky bluegrass and perennial ryegrass also reduces its occurrence. Resistant varieties of Kentucky bluegrass include 'Adelphi', 'Columbia', 'Enmundi', 'Glade', 'Parade', and 'Sydsport'.

Fenarimol, iprodione, and triadimefon control summer patch.

Necrotic Ring Spot
Spring to fall
This disease is a variation of summer patch that usually occurs where temperatures are cool. It also produces "frog-eye" patterns with small circles of dead grass surrounding a tuft of green grass. Infected leaves turn reddish purple.

This fungus is active at relatively low temperatures (58° to 82° F), but the dead spots may not become apparent until warm, dry periods in summer, when they suddenly appear.

Kentucky bluegrass is the most susceptible, particularly the varieties 'Arboretum', 'Fylking', 'Park', and 'Pennstar'. Bentgrass, creeping bentgrass, and fine fescues are also susceptible. No resistant grasses have been identified.

Cultural controls are the same as those for summer patch. Fenarimol or iprodione, along with applications of nitrogen, can check the growth of necrotic ring spot.

Take-All Patch
Late spring and early fall
Sometimes called ophiobolus patch, this fungal disease thrives only in the cool, moist coastal regions of the Pacific Northwest. It first appears as small, brown spots that may enlarge quickly.

Bentgrass is the most commonly damaged grass, but Kentucky bluegrass and ryegrass may also be bothered. All fescues are resistant.

The best cultural control is to grow a lawn in slightly acid soil. When the problem becomes severe, apply 2 pounds of sulfur per 1,000 square feet of lawn, and water it in. Alternatively, try an acid-forming fertilizer, such as ammonium sulfate. Controlling the disease with fungicides is difficult.

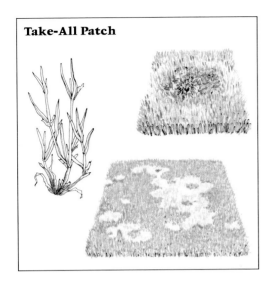

Take-All Patch

Typhula Blight

Typhula Blight

In snow

Also known as gray snow mold, this fungal disease first appears as light yellow to grayish white circular areas at the time of spring thawing. Affected patches are a few inches to a few feet in diameter. The dead grass may be covered with a grayish fungal growth. Typhula blight occurs primarily in the northern United States and Canada, not reaching as far south as fusarium patch.

A deep snow cover that is slow to melt is prime breeding ground for this fungus. The mold begins to grow at temperatures just above freezing and achieves optimum growth at 48° to 55° F. Almost all cool-season grasses are vulnerable.

To help prevent typhula blight, be sure the lawn is not overfertilized with nitrogen before the first snowfall. Avoid excessive use of lime. Keep the thatch layer to a minimum. Rake the grass in early spring to break up matting and promote drying. Fertilize lightly in early spring to stimulate growth.

Since typhula blight is found mainly in spots where snow lingers (such as against a house or garage), these areas may be the only ones needing treatment. Apply anilazine, chloroneb, chlorothalonil, fenarimol, iprodione, or triadimefon in fall before the first snowfall.

CULTURAL PROBLEMS

Some problems may persist in your lawn even after you have conscientiously eliminated weeds, pests, and diseases. Some are caused by processes beyond your control, such as the natural dormancy periods of certain grasses; others are symptoms of an environmental or maintenance problem, such as poor drainage or too much fertilizer. If uncorrected, cultural problems can encourage diseases or pests to take hold.

If your lawn shows any of the symptoms listed here, do not despair. Most lawns are resilient and can easily survive the majority of these problems.

Chemical Burn

Many lawns are damaged by spilled fertilizer, herbicide, gasoline, or dog urination. Chemical burn is characterized by distinct patches of dead grass. Bright green grass surrounding a patch of dead grass is typical of burns from fertilizer and dog urination; both are caused by an abundance of nitrogen. Several treatments can help prevent this damage if you act soon after the exposure. For water-soluble material (most herbicides, fertilizers, and urine), thoroughly drench the soil with water. For water-insoluble material (gasoline or oil), first drench the soil with soapy water (about the consistency of dishwater), then water thoroughly. For herbicides containing triazine, remove the burned grass and the soil underneath and work activated charcoal into the dead spot. In all cases, once the symptoms appear it is too late to save the grass. If the burned area is small, surrounding grass may fill it in. If that fails, replace the soil under dead spots and patch damaged areas. See page 108 for instructions on patching.

Dry Spots

Many lawns dry out unevenly after a rain or watering. Frequent dry spots include areas of compacted soil, fast-draining patches in an otherwise slow-draining yard, and places that the sprinkler has missed. The grasses in these water-starved areas may change from bright to dull green, sometimes creating the false impression that insects or diseases are present. To confirm the diagnosis of water stress, walk across the lawn. If your footprints do not spring back reasonably soon, dryness is the problem. In lawns of cool-season grass, raise the cutting height at least ½ inch and water deeply. Check the soil moisture occasionally with a soil probe or moisture meter. If one area begins to show signs of drought, use a portable sprinkler or a handheld hose to soak the area. Warm-season grasses are less troubled by drought and are slower to show its effects; however, the treatment for these grasses is the same.

Low Spots with Drainage Problems

Low spots in most lawns are caused by either careless grading at the time of planting, or soil movement or erosion in the mature lawn. Rotting wood, buried beneath the soil, can also cause low spots as it decomposes. Pools of standing water can cause the low spots to sink even farther.

If a low spot is not very obvious, you can fill it in gradually by spreading small amounts of soil or sand over the low area, allowing the grass to grow up through it until the lawn reaches the level of the surrounding turf.

If the drainage problem is more widespread or severe, first try to alleviate it by deeply aerating the wet patch with a plugging aerator or by hand. It is best to wait for the soil to dry out before attempting this. This should allow water to penetrate farther down into the soil. Then use a sod cutter (a motorized tool available from equipment rental companies) to cut out and roll back the turf in the low area. Add enough soil to the newly bare patch to bring it up to the level of the surrounding lawn. Then roll the grass back into place and tamp it down.

Nitrogen or Iron Deficiency

Nitrogen is the nutrient needed by lawns in the greatest quantity. The actual amount varies with the type of grass and with other conditions such as temperature or watering, but most grasses need some lawn fertilizer containing nitrogen every year. If you have not been applying fertilizer, your lawn is probably slightly yellow and not growing as well as it should be. See pages 67 to 73 for information on fertilizing.

If you have fertilized adequately and the lawn is still yellow and growing slowly, the problem could be a lack of iron or a pH level that is too high. Some grasses, such as centipedegrass, are especially sensitive to the lack of iron. Apply iron either as a liquid spray or in combination with nitrogen and sulfur. For information about pH problems, see page 30.

Scalping and Dull Mower Injury

Lawn scalping occurs whenever too much grass is cut off at one time, or whenever high spots are shaved bare by the mower. Removing more than one third of the lawn's height at one time creates a severe shock to the grass, and the exposed lower white portions of the grass blades will soon turn brown.

Chemical Burn

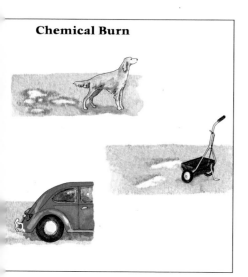

Dry Spots

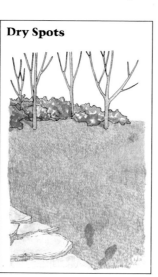

Low Spots with Drainage Problems

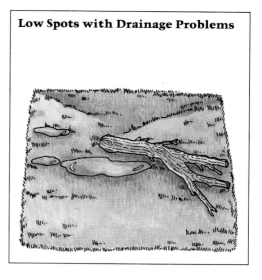

Grass will normally grow back after being scalped, but those areas mowed too low will take some time to recover. If scalping occurs often when you mow, set your mower a bit higher than normal.

Mowing your lawn with dull blades gives the lawn a grayish cast a day or so later. This happens because the leaf tips are shredded instead of cut, and turn brown. The effect is especially noticeable in dry weather. Besides being unsightly, shredded tips make an easy entry point for many disease organisms. Sharpen mower blades on a regular basis.

Trees in the Lawn

Grass can survive under a tree if at least half the sunlight striking the top of the tree filters through to the lawn. If the shade under trees is just over 50 percent, some tree trimming may be all it takes to allow a lawn to thrive. Proceed with caution, however, since tree trimming is expensive and you may discover that the problem has a different cause, such as an accumulation of thatch or dead leaves.

By far the easiest way to grow a lawn in any shady environment is to plant the area with a shade-tolerant grass. Many lawn seed mixtures contain seeds for both sun-loving and shade-tolerant varieties. Each variety eventually dominates the area where it is best adapted. You can also buy special shady-lawn seed mixtures.

If the shade is so intense that grass grows sparsely or not at all, consider planting another ground cover such as ajuga, creeping myrtle, ivy, or pachysandra. All of these will tolerate light foot traffic. As an alternative to using

plants, try covering the area with an attractive mulch of stone or bark.

Trees in the lawn can create several problems in addition to excess shade. Tree roots can compete with lawn roots for the available water and nutrients in the soil. To remedy this, give the soil under large trees an extra-deep soaking (from 2 to 6 feet deep, depending on the size and type of tree) two or three times a year, so that they can receive the water they need. A root waterer (a yard-long hollow probe that channels liquids into the soil from a hose) can also be used to get nutrients down below the roots of lawn grasses.

A tree growing in a lawn sometimes pushes one or more of its roots above the surface. At best, mowing becomes difficult; at worst, the tree or the mower blades are damaged.

If the root is slender, it can be removed. Using a shovel, cut into the lawn on both sides of the root. Peel away the turf and carefully chop out the root with a pickax or mattock. Finally, roll the turf back into place and firm it down.

If a root is too large to deal with in this way, the best plan is to remove the lawn from the root. With a pickax or mattock, simply cut out the grass around the root and replace it with a bed of other plants. Where this is not possible, another alternative is to add soil to form a gently sloping 2-inch mound over the length of the root. Firm down this soil and then plant over it with grass seed or sod.

Fallen leaves and other debris can present yet another problem for lawns. If allowed to accumulate on the grass, they can smother it and may eventually kill it. In cool-season areas,

Nitrogen or Iron Deficiency

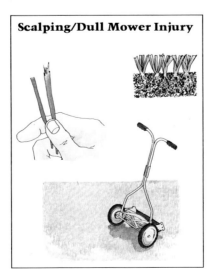

Scalping/Dull Mower Injury

Trees in the Lawn

A damaged section of lawn can be cut out and patched with a piece of sod. Be sure to use the same kind of grass.

an autumn covering of dead leaves robs grasses of the light they need to produce rhizomes and to build reserves of food for the winter. In addition, leaf litter is often very acidic and can alter soil pH, making it more difficult for some grasses to grow. Leaves left on the grass can also harbor insects and diseases.

The best solution is to remove the leaves with a lawn rake, yard vacuum, or power blower, and place them in a compost bin or put them out with the trash. Any fallen branches or fruit should also be removed from the lawn and hauled away.

REPAIRING A DAMAGED LAWN

When damage occurs to a growing lawn, whether through disease, infestation, chemical burning, drought, or heavy wear, the first step is to remove the source of the problem. That accomplished, you will need to repair the damaged areas.

If damage is confined to small spots, it may be enough to dig up and patch the affected areas. However, if the problem affects the whole lawn and cannot be reversed by routine measures such as aeration (see page 75) or dethatching (see page 76), you may find that it is time to renovate the lawn.

It is wise to consult a lawn care professional before starting any large-scale repair project. You may find that the problem can be solved by less drastic measures, or that it is so great that it is best handled professionally.

Patching

There are often small spots in the lawn, perhaps burned by chemicals or choked by weeds, that need replacing. Patching involves removing the damaged section and replacing it either with a piece of sod or by reseeding, resprigging, or replugging. The patched section should closely match the type of grass that is growing in the rest of the lawn. Many nurseries normally stock a small amount of sod just for use in patching.

Dig out the damaged area with a shovel or trowel and loosen the soil underneath. If spilled gasoline or herbicide is the cause of the dead spot, remove several inches of the soil and replace it. (For more information on spills, see page 105.) Bring the underlying soil to proper grade and cut a piece of sod to fit.

If you are patching with seed, sprigs, or plugs, follow the same procedure as for any new planting. Regardless of the planting method, treat patched areas as you would a new lawn. Remember that careful watering is important to help the patched area become established (see the watering guidelines for new lawns on page 54 and in the second chapter).

Renovating

Renovating a lawn consists of killing the existing grass and replacing it with new grass. It is usually performed when a lawn has been devastated by insects or disease, has sustained cumulative damage from soil compaction, or suffers from a serious chronic problem such as poor drainage. A lawn that has been in place for a long time may simply have deteriorated badly, making replacement the most practical alternative. A lawn might also be renovated so that a new kind of grass can be planted, perhaps to provide better tolerance to drought or wear, or greater resistance to a troublesome pest or disease.

While you are renovating, you can take the opportunity to cultivate and amend the soil, adjust the grade, install an underground irrigation system, and relandscape.

Lawn renovation has become more routine than it once was, thanks to two innovations: the development of the herbicide glyphosate, which kills the lawn rapidly and breaks down quickly into a harmless residue, and the advent of improved varieties of lawn grass. These new cultivars offer such great improvements over existing grasses (for example, slower growth, better shade or drought tolerance) that it is often well worth the trouble of removing an existing lawn in order to grow them.

Renovating a lawn is a fairly major undertaking. It takes time and effort and may involve the use of heavy equipment. It also entails some cost for seed, sprigs, plugs, or sod, and for soil amendments. The specialized equipment used for renovation can be rented from local nurseries, hardware stores, and equipment rental companies; you may also need to rent or borrow a vehicle to haul away the debris.

Because renovating a lawn is normally an arduous job, you may choose to have professionals do it for you. If you do, make sure that the people you hire are experienced at this procedure and possess the necessary equipment. Also make certain that they will plant the variety of grass you want in place of your old lawn.

Removing the old lawn   The task of removing a lawn has two phases: killing the old grass and clearing it away. The herbicide glyphosate, which is the active ingredient in several commercial products, is a relatively low-hazard chemical that interferes with amino acid synthesis in plants to kill both lawn grasses and weeds. Once in the soil, glyphosate quickly becomes inactive, allowing the lawn to be replanted within a few hours. Normally, however, gardeners wait a week or two to make sure that no difficult weeds have been missed. In dry climates, watering during this period will encourage surviving weed seeds to germinate. If any weeds persist, the weed killer can be applied again as a spot treatment.

Once the old lawn and all weeds are dead, the next step is to clear the soil of this material, including thatch, so that seeds will be able to germinate properly. The more material that covers the soil, the more intensive the clearing procedure must be.

If there is little or no thatch, you can simply slice through the thin layer of dead material with a vertical mower, a fixed-blade dethatcher, an overseeder, a slit seeder, a slicer, or a groover. These devices are usually available from equipment rental companies. Vertical mowers and fixed-blade dethatchers are the types most often used by homeowners. Each type of machine cuts through the dead matter and makes slits in the soil. The key is to make slits ¼ inch or less through the dead material and into the soil about 1 to 2 inches apart.

If the layer of thatch and dead material is thicker than ¼ to ½ inch, simply slicing through it will not be enough to enable seeds to make good contact with the soil. The seeds will simply sit on top of the thatch rather than make their way down through the narrow slits. In this case, rent a flail dethatcher to perform a more severe dethatching, setting it to cut to the soil level. The machine finely chops the thatch material, which is then raked or vacuumed off, leaving just enough for a light mulch. If the lawn is large or has a lot of thatch, you can expect to haul off substantial amounts of debris from this operation. The lawn is then sliced with an overseeder, slicer, or groover as described above.

If you will be taking remedial action such as adding compost and other soil amendments, improving drainage, installing an underground irrigation system, or relandscaping, do this now. After regrading the new soil surface (page 32), use a slicer or slitter to create grooves in the soil to roughen its surface for planting.

Planting the new lawn   After the ground has been cleared and any repairs or relandscaping accomplished, seed the lawn area with a rotary spreader, or plant sprigs, plugs, or sod (see pages 36 to 45). If you have cut away the lawn completely rather than slicing or flailing it, rake the soil lightly to cover the seed. Then spread a thin layer of good topsoil, compost, manure, or other top-dressing material over the newly planted lawn and keep it well watered.

It is not always easy to decide whether to sow seeds into slits in the dead lawn, to dethatch severely, or to use a sod cutter. If in doubt, use the next most rigorous procedure.

U.S. Measure and Metric Measure Conversion Chart

	Symbol	When you know:	Multiply by:	To find:	Rounded Measures for Quick Reference		
Mass (Weight)	oz	ounces	28.35	grams	1 oz		= 30 g
	lb	pounds	0.45	kilograms	4 oz		= 115 g
	g	grams	0.035	ounces	8 oz		= 225 g
	kg	kilograms	2.2	pounds	16 oz	= 1 lb	= 450 g
					32 oz	= 2 lb	= 900 g
					36 oz	= 2¼ lb	= 1000 g (1 kg)
Volume	pt	pints	0.47	liters	1 c	= 8 oz	= 250 ml
	qt	quarts	0.95	liters	2 c (1 pt)	= 16 oz	= 500 ml
	gal	gallons	3.785	liters	4 c (1 qt)	= 32 oz	= 1 liter
	ml	milliliters	0.034	fluid ounces	4 qt (1 gal)	= 128 oz	= 3¾ liter
Length	in.	inches	2.54	centimeters	⅜ in.	= 1 cm	
	ft	feet	30.48	centimeters	1 in.	= 2.5 cm	
	yd	yards	0.9144	meters	2 in.	= 5 cm	
	mi	miles	1.609	kilometers	2½ in.	= 6.5 cm	
	km	kilometers	0.621	miles	12 in. (1 ft)	= 30 cm	
	m	meters	1.094	yards	1 yd	= 90 cm	
	cm	centimeters	0.39	inches	100 ft	= 30 m	
					1 mi	= 1.6 km	
Temperature	°F	Fahrenheit	⁵⁄₉ (after subtracting 32)	Celsius	32° F	= 0° C	
	°C	Celsius	⁹⁄₅ (then add 32)	Fahrenheit	212° F	= 100° C	
Area	in.²	square inches	6.452	square centimeters	1 in.²	= 6.5 cm²	
	ft²	square feet	929.0	square centimeters	1 ft²	= 930 cm²	
	yd²	square yards	8361.0	square centimeters	1 yd²	= 8360 cm²	
	a.	acres	0.4047	hectares	1 a.	= 4050 m²	

Formulas for Exact Measures